ROCKED

ROCKED

*How to Respond When Life's Circumstances
Rock You to Your Core*

JOE CHAMPION

CROSS
BOOKS

CrossBooks™
A Division of LifeWay
1663 Liberty Drive
Bloomington, IN 47403
www.crossbooks.com
Phone: 1-866-879-0502

First published by CrossBooks 4/19/2010

ISBN: 978-1-6150-7220-0 (sc)

Library of Congress Control Number: 2010905260

Printed in the United States of America
Bloomington, Indiana

This book is printed on acid-free paper.

CONTENTS

INTRODUCTION

*I*n the late afternoon of January 2, 2010, the island nation of Haiti was rocked to its core. An earthquake landing on the Richter scale at 7.0 magnitude began under the capital city of Port-au-Prince and radiated out, devastating everything in its reach for miles and miles and miles. The death toll at the time I'm writing this has risen over 200,000. Thousands upon thousands more are injured, homeless, or both.

We can sit in our comfortable homes from the safety of our own country and watch on TV the agony on the faces of the people of Haiti, hear the desperation and the pain in their voices, and feel sympathy for them. We are sad when we see what has happened there, and we naturally want to help. Thousands of Christians already are. But let's not kid ourselves. We are not safe. Our comfort is temporary.

At any given minute, we can experience a devastating earthquake of our own.

Of course, the catastrophe you and I face will probably not be in the form of a literal earthquake. But if you've lived for any substantial length of time on this earth, you know you're only a heartbeat away from a devastating phone call, a devastating email or letter, a devastating announcement from a spouse or child or friend or boss. It may come from the bank. It may come from your church. It may come from your own body, announcing to you in sudden symptoms that something is terribly wrong inside.

We are only a heartbeat away from being rocked to our core.

It usually comes as a surprise when it happens, but the fact that it happens should be no surprise. Jesus himself said to his followers in John 16:33, "Here on earth you will have many trials and sorrows."

There it is, straight from our Lord's mouth. If you're gonna live, you're gonna have trouble. If you're gonna live, you're gonna go through some really difficult times. If you want to live victoriously—in your family life, in your business, in your marriage, in your spiritual growth—you have to accept the fact that nobody gets to victory without struggle. But while we may not know when our world is going to be rocked, we can be prepared for when it is.

What do you do when your spouse says it's over? What do you do when your boss says your services are no longer needed? What do you do when your friends bail on you? What do you do when your house is foreclosed on, when your child gets cancer, when your loved one dies, when the doctors say it's serious? What do you do when the storms of life show up unannounced and take your home, your family, or your health?

Throughout this book we're going to look at the life of Job, a man who had it all and had it all taken away. Job was someone who had his world rocked, totally. If you have ever been there, or if you want to be prepared for that time to come when you may be there, you can find no greater encouragement and no greater assurance than this powerful story from God's word. Over the next seven chapters, we are going to explore God's purposes for pain and the practical help He gives us to make our way through it, into radical success over it, and radical trust of God in it.

You might be facing a devastating situation right now. Maybe just recently you found yourself at the epicenter of an earthquake that has shaken your very life. You feel vulnerable, scared, angry, confused. You may be struggling with doubt. Maybe you just need to hear clearly from God that He loves you and has plans for how to prosper you in and through your pain. My hope is to share with you that God does care for you and that He does have a purpose for you, especially when you're rocked to your foundations.

Take heart!

CHAPTER ONE

TAKEN BY SURPRISE

S ometimes our world comes crashing down. Here, in her own words, is the voice of Dawn, a woman in our congregation, whose world came crashing down in an instant:

> Well, I thought I was pregnant. I mean, I had the nausea, everything. I had people coming up to me telling me I had a glow. And some people flat out asked me, "Are you pregnant?" And so when I found out what it was, it was a little, you know, shocking. My first ultrasound, my husband was with me, and they said this looks like a molar pregnancy. And I said, "I have no idea what that is." I was sent back to the waiting room with a bunch of paperwork that said congratulations on your new baby. And I was sitting there

thinking, *I don't even know if I have a baby.* I don't even know if this is a typical baby. I knew nothing. When they said the word oncology, that's when I just lost it. I conceived a tumor."

This young lady went into the doctor's office expecting to find out she was going to have a child, expecting to leave ready to pick out baby names and colors for the nursery. Instead she found out she had cancer. She went in looking forward to bringing forth life but came out fighting for her own. She went in with hope yet found despair. This young lady had her world rocked.

This is what it means to be rocked. This is what it means to be hit, surprised by a sudden circumstance that shakes you to the core, and to have no answers.

What do you do when *you're* rocked? What happens when your *world* is rocked, physically, spiritually, emotionally, or all of the above? How do you respond?

The truth is your response will make all the difference between hope and despair, between wallowing or surviving or even prevailing. You cannot avoid having your world rocked. In Ecclesiastes 3:1-4, we learn that there is a time to die, to uproot, to kill, to tear down, to weep, and to mourn. Life runs in seasons, Ecclesiastes tells us. Just as there are times for laughing and dancing, times of peace and joy, there are going to be times of sadness, disappointment and daunting challenges.

Even Jesus said, "In this world, you will have trouble" (John 16:33). This means that if you're alive, you're going to go through some difficult things. Jesus knew what He was talking about. He stated the fact, but we need to have an answer. We need to know what to do when the trouble comes. The good news is that God shows us how to respond when our world is rocked. Jesus does not leave us hanging. When He says, "In this world, you will have trouble," He follows it up with, "But take heart! I have overcome the world." This means that Jesus, the Rock Himself, is bigger and stronger and more powerful than any circumstances that will rock our lives. He is more powerful than the hardest of times and the hardest of hearts. The Bible is full of God speaking into lives that have been rocked.

God's desire is for us to live free of fear and full of faith, even as the walls around us crumble. God calls us to cry out *from experience*. David said, "My God is my rock, in whom I take refuge, my shield and the horn of my salvation. He is my stronghold, my refuge and my

Savior" (2 Samuel 22:3). While the world around us is always changing, God remains the same.

You may be facing insurmountable odds, inconceivable disaster, or incredible pain, but God has brought this message to you to encourage you, to remind you of your future and your hope.

The Man Who Lost Everything

I sometimes wish the book of Job wasn't in the Bible. I just don't like it. But I'm glad it's there, because I also don't like when worlds are rocked. I don't like to hear about people having cancer. I don't like to hear about people losing their health, losing their business, losing their strength, losing their loved ones.

The book of Job is the story of a man who lost everything. (Well, everything except for a nagging wife and discouraging friends!) He lost his children, his home, his finances, his resources, and his health. The Bible tells us he didn't do anything to deserve the special treatment of suffering. We all deserve suffering, because we're all sinners, but there was nothing about Job's life that required special hardship because of extraordinary sin or failing. In fact, the story is quick to point out that Job was "blameless and upright," that "he feared God and turned away from evil" (Job 1:1). It tells us this not so that we'll see how awesome Job is, but so that we'll know that suffering happens to *everyone*, awesome or not.

In fact, the greatness of Job—the man who lost everything—is not in how he was before his world was rocked, but how he was *afterward*. The greatness of Job is found in his clinging to the greatness of God in the midst of his pain and suffering and lack of understanding. As the rains came and the winds blew and the house came crashing down, Job was a man who remained on a firm foundation. Throughout this book, we will be taking detours into the book of Job.

God gives us the book of Job in the Bible because He knows we are going to go through some serious pain in our lives. Jesus' promise in John 16:33 is very clear: it's not *if* our world will be rocked—it's *when*. In one of His sermons, Jesus gives this warning through a simple story:

> Therefore everyone who hears these words of mine and puts them into practice is like a wise man who built his house on the rock. The rain came down, the streams rose, and the winds blew and beat against that house; yet it did not

fall, because it had its foundation on the rock. But everyone who hears these words of mine and does not put them into practice is like a foolish man who built his house on sand. The rain came down, the streams rose, and the winds blew and beat against that house, and it fell with a great crash.

(Matthew 7:24-27)

In children's church we turn this story into a cute little song. What's happening in this story is not cute. It's a story for grown-ups. The rain of bankruptcy comes down. The streams of an adulterous marriage rise. The winds of cancer blow and beat. Worlds fall apart often, and usually it happens "with a great crash."

Job can be for us what Jesus prescribes at the beginning of his illustration. Words that are put into practice provide a firm foundation.

You and I don't get the option of exempting ourselves from trouble. There's no easy pass through life. But we do get the option of how we respond to our troubles. We do have the opportunity to learn how to handle situations that rock our world.

That One Fateful Day

If you maintain substantial financial investments, and if your life and your finances are connected, you know the difference a day can make. Several hundred points either way on the Dow Jones can rock your world. You know a day can make years of difference.

Maybe you don't give two cents about the stock exchange, but I know everyone has experienced the difference a day makes. One day life is routine, normal. The next day, your world is rocked by scandal. You had no idea things had become so bad, but your spouse wants out of your marriage. Maybe you've been rocked by information at work. Out of the blue, you find a pink slip in your box. You went into work ready to conquer the day, but they just want you to pack up your stuff and leave.

There are millions of people in America right now who look like they have it all together. Everything is beautiful. The home is wonderfully landscaped, the sprinkler heads spray the yard with rainbows like clockwork, 2.5 kids play happily with energetic pets. But inside their hearts, their lives are falling apart. If it's not financial ruin, marital ruin, or medical ruin, it's emotional ruin. Millions suffer from a depression and a discouragement they have no explanation for, which only makes it worse.

So often this all happens like someone has flipped a switch. The world has just arbitrarily turned suffering on. The setting of your life has been switched from "Peace" to "Rocked."

For this reason, we should not be surprised when we are surprised.

Hardship comes to us like it came to Job. It comes once. It comes twice. It comes three times. It comes four times. It comes like a flood. Have you ever had that happen to you? It's just one thing after another? It is as if life itself is boxing with you, like there's no jab that isn't followed with an uppercut?

Suffering can come like a sudden flood. It is interesting to think about floods coming suddenly. We tend to think that one could see a flood coming. Many who have witnessed the devastation of flash floods testify otherwise. Approximately one-tenth of America is made up of floodplains that are able to handle inordinate amounts of water thanks to man-made levees and other controls. But every now and then, in a flash, nature dishes something out that is so beyond the norm, it can hardly be anticipated. On June 14, 1903, for instance, a storm of rain and hail that is said to have lasted only one hour in the Blue Mountains of Oregon sent a 20-foot wave down into the town of Heppner, washing away 200 people and killing 324. A one-hour storm. On one day. Hundreds dead.

More recently, on December 26, 2004, an undersea earthquake caused a tsunami in the Indian Ocean that eventually killed 230,000 men, women, and children in more than 4 countries. These people were working, playing, and sleeping. Suddenly, a gigantic flood came and wiped them out.

Suddenly. On one fateful day, it just shows up, and it usually keeps on coming. (By some estimates, the Indian Ocean tsunami went on to indirectly cause the death of another 700,000 people!)

Notice how the rocking of Job's world begins in Job 1:13, "One day . . ." It all came down. Like a flash flood, like a tsunami of suffering, it all suddenly seemed to happen.

The rest of the report informs us that Job's sons and daughters were eating and drinking wine in their oldest brother's house, minding their own business when tragedy struck.

> [A] messenger came to Job and said, "The oxen were plowing and the donkeys were grazing nearby, and the Sabeans attacked and carried them off. They put the servants to the sword, and I am the only one who has escaped to tell you!"
>
> While he was still speaking, another messenger came and said, "The fire of God fell from the sky and burned up the sheep and the servants, and I am the only one who has escaped to tell you!"
>
> While he was still speaking, another messenger came and said, "The Chaldeans formed three raiding parties and swept down on your camels and carried them off. They put the servants to the sword, and I am the only one who has escaped to tell you!"
>
> While he was still speaking, yet another messenger came and said, "Your sons and daughters were feasting and drinking wine at the oldest brother's house, when suddenly a mighty wind swept in from the desert and struck the four corners of the house. It collapsed on them and they are dead, and I am the only one who has escaped to tell you!"
>
> (Job 1:13-19)

All of a sudden, it's one thing after another. And one thing worse than the one before it.

So Job lost his oxen dealership. Now, he's lost his sheep dealership. And then his camel dealership. And while he is in shock that he's lost basically his entire business and all the resources that go with it, he suffers the harshest blow of all: he is told his sons and daughters were eating and drinking wine in their oldest brother's house and suddenly a great wind, tornado-like, hurricane-like, came from across the wilderness out of nowhere and struck the four corners of the house and it fell on them.

Many of you reading this have lost a child. You know what it is like to mourn the loss of a life not yet fully lived. I don't have to ask you to imagine what it would be like for Job to lose everything . . . and then lose everything that really mattered—his children in the prime of their lives. You remember what it was like to not know pain one day and then know it intimately the next.

In one day for Job it came crashing down. Why did Job's world collapse? Job loved the Lord. He hated evil. In fact, the prophet, Ezekiel describes him as righteous (Ezekiel 14:14) and James commends his perseverance (James 5:11). The Bible would describe Job as a man who was so concerned about his family being right with God that if he knew that they were partying out late at the older brother's house, he would go make an animal sacrifice. He would say, "Now, Lord, I know my kids love to sow a little wild oats, but would you please forgive them?"

Many of your parents or grandparents were praying for you while you were out partying. While you were out making a mess of your life and doing some things you weren't supposed to be doing, maybe you had a Job at the house praying, "Oh, God, forgive them and cleanse them from all their sins." That was Job's character. He was a great man and a great parent. He was a guy who was actively concerned about his family's physical and spiritual well-being. The sudden loss of his family could not be written off because of his failure to care about them or pray for them.

The flood of suffering doesn't care who you are or what you do or how undeserving of it you think you are. Its job is to destroy. On the fateful day the flood came in your life, how did you respond? If it hasn't come yet, Jesus promises it will. How do you think you *will* respond?

Of all the people who did not deserve to have their world rocked, Job takes the top prize. In fact, until this "one day," Job didn't even know what it was to be rocked. He had built so big a hedge of protection around his family, he hadn't had the opportunity to face difficult times.

The Bible clearly says in Hebrews 12 that everything that can be shaken will be shaken. In other words, everything that can be rocked will be rocked (Hebrews 12:26-27). 2 Peter 3:10 says, "The heavens will disappear with a roar; the elements will be destroyed by fire, and the earth and everything in it will be laid bare." And so you and I are not to live unaware of those impending "one fateful days" of our lives. On that future day, everything that can be shaken will be shaken. You and I are not to be caught napping.

Unsurprised by the Surprises

Now you may want to say, "Joe, I wanted to read this book for some encouragement. Aren't you just putting fear into my heart?" My aim is not to scare you with what *could* be, but sober you with what *will* be. I do want to tell you what the Apostle Paul told his original readers in 2 Corinthians 1, which is that he doesn't want them to be uninformed—some translations say "ignorant"—of the hardship he was facing. I don't want you to be ignorant about the trouble that will come. We may be ignorant of the specific trouble itself until it arrives, but we don't need to be ignorant about trouble or what God says about it or what He wants to do in us and through us with it.

This is the idea behind what Paul is saying. *At times, things just seemingly fall apart. You don't go looking for failure, but it finds you anyway.* I believe Paul is urging us not to be caught unaware. I don't want to be ignorant about the fact that life brings pain, that hurting is part of the human experience. I don't want to be surprised by the surprises of suffering, and in fact, I want to be *unsurprised* as an act of Christian preparation.

There is often no rhyme or reason to the storms life brings our way. What you don't see in his letters is Paul struggling with trying to figure it all out. He rarely, if ever, asks or explains the *why* behind suffering. (And as the late musician Rich Mullins sang, "I know it wouldn't hurt any less, even if it could be explained.") Paul just says *it happens*. It doesn't really matter why. Even if you knew why, it wouldn't stop the storms from happening or keep them from causing damage. All the science in the world hasn't stopped earthquakes, even as we figure out all the science involved in what causes them. All the warning systems in the world can't move a million people in the matter of minutes it can take for a tsunami to make landfall.

All of a sudden, Job endures wave after wave after wave of attack. Paul says this is what happened to him, as well. "We were under great pressure, far beyond our ability to endure, so that we despaired even of life," he says (2 Corinthians 1:8). In other words, the pressure was stronger than his own strength. The floodwaters were too high and too swift to swim in and swim against. The flood of suffering was so difficult, he thought he was going to drown. He "despaired even of life."

Been there? Done that?

Maybe you've been through the surprise of suffering, felt even as though you've had a death sentence placed over you—on your life with cancer, on your livelihood because of unemployment and bankruptcy and debt, or your marriage because of infidelity or divorce. Maybe you've even been depressed about living itself.

However, if you look closely, maybe you've also been surprised by how resilient as a child of God you can be. Maybe you've looked back over those times and seen God's purpose at work in them. Maybe you've been surprised not just by suffering but by God's strength in you during your suffering.

In the midst of a world rocked by pain, do not trust in yourself, but in the God who can raise the dead. He is more than able and all-powerful. He can deliver you through anything and is able to keep your head above the waters. He can and is willing to help you.

Do not be surprised by suffering. However, when you suffer, do not be surprised that the Spirit of the Lord is on your side.

Throughout this book, you're going to learn some things from people like Job and Paul and from the modern lives of people like them, and like *you*. The stories about God's faithfulness are innumerable. You're going to learn what to do when you are faced with a world that's been rocked.

In this world, you will have your life rocked. But take heart! The Rock of our salvation has overcome the world.

CHAPTER TWO

CHOICES

"*E*veryday I had a choice to make. I could either be bitter about the fact that I could no longer have my own children, or I could be joyful."

Those are words from Dawn, whose story you were introduced to in the previous chapter. When our world is rocked, will we be bitter? Will we somehow find some way to be joyful? This is not an easy choice, but it is a choice that we are all faced with.

So how do you do it? How do you "take heart?" What is your natural inclination? Is it bitterness or joy? Is it despair or hope?

In the midst of your confusion, do you hold on tight to your faith?

A Faithful "Why?"

Usually the first question we ask is "Why, God?" Our first inclination is to go to the reason, the explanation. Our first move is to look for the place to lay the blame. We want to know "Why is this happening?" We wonder, "What is causing this?" It just seems logical. If there is an effect, there must be a cause, some kind of inward reason.

We live in a fallen world. Sometimes there is no other reason than that. There are times we can't plan and there are seasons we can't anticipate and there are events that simply have no explanation. Because of the fall, things just . . . fall. God says in the person of Christ, "He causes His sun to rise on the evil and the good, and sends rain on the righteous and the unrighteous" (Matthew 5:45). This means the sun shines on bad people and the rain falls on good people, not because people are good or bad, but because the sun shines and the rain falls. In the Psalms, David is constantly asking God why bad people are prospering while good people are suffering. This isn't a new problem. We naturally want to know, "Why do bad things happen to good people?" The Bible tells us that Job was blameless and upright. So we know that sometimes terrible things happen to us despite our efforts to obey God, love others, and be good in the world.

Job asked a lot of "why" questions. But he also said, "Though He slay me, yet will I hope in Him" (Job 13:15).

In the midst of his confusion and in the pain of his grief and suffering, Job chose to trust. He chose the faithful "why?" not a despairing, hopeless "why?"

You and I can get to that place of hope and joy when the world around us is being rocked to its core. We can respond with hope like Job.

Two Choices in the Pain

You and I don't have a choice about whether we're going to experience pain or not. We don't get to choose whether we will be rocked or not. It just happens. But we *do* get to choose how we respond in that pain.

Here is the rest of Dawn's story:

> I took a hit physically. I mean, it was tough. I have had a partial hysterectomy and six months of chemotherapy. I have hard days.

I'm just tired or nauseous or, you know, hair loss and all of the real things that come with chemotherapy. But I think it's human nature to ask "Why? Why did this happen?" or "Is God in this?" I asked why for about a day. I grieved for about a day. And then I realized it's really counterproductive to do that. I believe that when Jesus died on the cross, he took our sicknesses with our sins. And it doesn't mean that we're never going to sin again any more than it means we're never going to be sick again. Because people are diagnosed with cancer all the time. I realized how crucial it is to have fellowship with the Lord every day, especially when you're going through a storm. You know, we need our brothers and sisters in Christ, and people were so encouraging. We had meals brought to us. My church family always spoke right to me, like "I have a really good scripture for you today," or "I thought of you in my quiet time," and they would speak scripture over me. And that was just priceless. And I guess I prefer to remember that the Lord is still sitting on a throne. He hasn't forgotten me. Last Friday was my last treatment. My blood work has been negative for four weeks. So praise God. It's behind me. I believe that he's healed me and that he'll restore my body.

That is what we call the perspective of faith. Dawn sees what cannot be seen and hoped for what she couldn't yet feel. But she believed God was in control and that he

cares for her. Because of her faith and the supr
local church, she chose joy.

There are similarities in her story and Job's story.
Although she only allowed herself to grieve and ask why
for one day, she didn't pretend she wasn't hurting.

1. When your world is rocked, don't hold it in.

When Job heard the news, when his world was rocked,
the Bible says that he rose, he tore his robe, he shaved his
head, and he fell to the ground.

Don't hold it in. In our good desire to not be irrational
or complain, we can make the bad decision of trying
to keep a lid on what's going on. In fact, I think that's
usually counterproductive. Holding it in doesn't do what
we think it will; it actually slows down how we process
our pain.

When we hold it in, we are going against the way
God has made us. Where do you think those tears
come from? Why are some of you reading this already
touched by Dawn's story? Where does that emotional
connection come from? It comes from God, who has
placed the ability to feel deeply inside each of us when
He created us.

So Job, when he gets the news, rips his shirt off. Of course, I'm not saying you should rip your shirt off right now. I'm not saying go home and shave your head like Job did. I'm not saying go home and do something destructive to your property. But I am telling you this: don't keep it in. It's okay to let it out.

Have you ever talked to someone who revealed a past hurt or time of intense pain and you said, "Wow, I never knew"? Or how often have you received news from someone about a divorce or a wayward family member, and you thought, "Man, I had no idea. I never would've guessed that could've happened to them"? We are taken by surprise when others reveal the trials of their past because when the trial was happening, they kept it hidden. But nobody can grieve with you and weep with you, as Romans 12:15 says, and nobody can support you, if you hold it in. When you hold it in, you prevent others from being God's instruments of healing in your life.

When I was a young youth pastor, I was in my first church. I had never performed a funeral. I had only attended one funeral in my life, and that was my dad's. But I was given news one night that a family connected to our church, with boys who had been in our youth group, had suffered an unbelievable tragedy. In the middle of the night, the dad, a corporate attorney for a large corporation in New Orleans, snapped. And he killed his two boys. Then he turned the gun on his wife and shot her in the head, and then turned the gun on himself.

Five days later I am doing not just *a* funeral, but I was doing three funerals. At the first funeral that I preached, I buried two teenage boys and their daddy who killed them. What do you say to a group of people gathered in this situation? What do you say to a family for whom their only grandkids, their only nephews, were these boys? What do you say to them without appearing to condemn the man in their family who has murdered them? What do you do when, as you're trying to figure out what to say, the news media is all over the place trying to learn more about the tragedy?

I didn't know. I didn't know what to say or do, really, because I didn't know any of the things leading up to this awful event were going on. Nobody else did either; it was kept a secret. This family kept a lid on their pain until the lid couldn't keep it in any more.

Do you know what Job did when his world was rocked? He went head first into God. He basically said,

"God, let me just tell you how I feel about this. I need help!" And he rips his shirt and he shaves his head. He allows himself to outwardly feel what he inwardly feels.

You and I have to learn to express ourselves before God. I'm not saying to break things. I'm not telling you to go drop a few verbal bombs on people, and say, "Well, Pastor Joe told me I need to get it out." But I *am* telling you this: before you explode, you need to communicate. The Bible tells us in James 5:16 to confess to one another.

When Jesus was under the strain of a world that was being rocked, when He knew He was about to go to the cross, He cried out. The Bible says in Hebrews 5:7 that Jesus "offered up prayers and petitions with loud cries and tears." Jesus prayed with expression. In His heart-wrenching prayer before He went to the cross, He said, "God, please, if there is any way possible, any other way that this can be handled, please do it" (Matthew 26:39). I really don't think He was sitting there peacefully with hands lightly clasped and a pleasant smile on His face. He was pouring His guts out. He was under such strain, that the Bible tells us He was sweating blood. Luke 22:24 says, "And being in anguish, He prayed more earnestly, and His sweat was like drops of blood falling to the ground." That is not an unfeeling prayer.

Your body has been designed by God to communicate to others what you're going through. You need to have a place where you can go and express yourself. You have that place with the people called the church. You have that place with God in prayer. You need these places. There it's okay to feel what you're feeling, to express yourself, and to ask "why?"

Jesus from the cross even says to the Father, "Why have you forsaken me?" (Mark 15:34). And He is echoing David in Psalm 22 crying out the same thing to God in his moment of pain. They asked why.

It's okay to let it out and ask why, but we need to learn to ask why without anger and bitterness. Dawn realized this. She said her bitterness was counterproductive. Job realized this when he says to his wife, who is nagging him to curse God, "Shall we accept good from God, and not trouble?" (Job 2:10). Even Hebrews 5:7, which says Jesus prayed loud, tearful prayers, says, "He was heard because of his reverent submission." And in His blood, sweat, and tears moments praying in the garden, after Jesus asks the

Father if a Plan B around suffering is available, He still says, "Your will be done, not mine."

It's okay to let it out. You *should* let it out. Be angry, even. Just don't get bitter. Jesus was hanging on the cross, dying an agonizing death, crying out to God, "Why have you forsaken me?" The soldiers who crucified Him tried to offer Him vinegar to drink to soothe His pain (John 19:29). Jesus didn't take the vinegar as if to say, "I'm not going to allow that gall, that bitterness in My mouth." It is fine to ask God why something is happening, or to ask Him to make it stop. Just make sure that you reject the bitterness that can so easily be justified when we go through intense times.

You can ask "why?" like Jesus asked "why?" but what we don't see in his *why* is an accusation against God. Jesus went full on into God and expressed himself, but he never blamed God. Job had many tearful conversations with God as he sorted through his pain and suffering, but he didn't blame God.

When I got the news one day that my son Jackson had to be rushed to the hospital, I remember being on the phone with my wife Lori, and the first thing I did—I guess it's a man thing—was hit my knee. It was reactive.

I was just feeling like, man, I've got to get this out. I thought about smashing our glass table, but I didn't want to sin and be destructive in my anger. The Bible says there is an expressive reaction to pain or suffering that is not sin. Ephesians 4:26 says to be angry but don't sin. I think Paul was saying, "Express your feelings, but don't sin."

Express. Don't hold it in. Talk about it. Because if you don't get it dealt with now, if you let it begin to boil, it will be harder to deal with later. Emotional anger unexpressed will lead to sinful bitterness.

When your world is rocked, don't suppress what you feel. You may not want to rip your shirt and fall to the ground like Job did, but you were created to talk it out. Follow Job's example and talk to God. There is healing in that process of talking and expressing, of getting it out. When you hold it in, it doesn't go away. In fact, it can hurt you more. The prophet Jeremiah says that when he held in his feelings, he became weary; he felt a fire in his bones (Jeremiah 20:9). Now, Jeremiah is talking about holding in the word of the Lord, but I believe there's a general principle reflected there. There are many doctors who will tell you, physiologically speaking, that if you try to hold on to that issue unexpressed in your life, it will begin to mage you in ways you didn't imagine. The emotional and psychological stress will have a physical effect. We already know how stress can lead to everything from headaches and ulcers to heart attacks. When you are in pain or trouble, you have to find an outlet of meaningful and honest expression.

2. When your world is rocked, don't stay alone.

What does Job do after he falls to the ground? The first thing he did was worship. In fact, Job 1:20 says he fell on the ground *to* worship. It's not like he fell down and thought, "Well, I might as well pray while I'm down here." No, his expression of pain, his dropping to the ground under the weight of having everything and everyone taken from him, was an act of worship itself.

Job worshiped in his pain. Do you know what this says about Job's response? It says that Job knew he could not be alone. In his submission to God he was expressing not just his hurt but his need to not be by himself.

The Psalms themselves, as full of wondering and asking and crying out in pain as the writers are, all serve as worship songs. The writers of the Psalms aren't crying out into nothingness. They are expressing themselves to a

God they believe is there. (Even when they're asking why he seems so distant.) Even as Job is expressing himself, he knows he is expressing himself to God. And the next thing that Job begins to do is realize he has to get in the presence of other people.

The worst thing that can happen when your world is rocked is to hunker down into some kind of solitude. Don't choose loneliness. Don't stay alone. As you see things happening to you and you feel a need to let it out, draw nearer to the Lord and come closer to your church family. The Bible says in Hebrews 10:25 that we should meet together and encourage each other more and more.

After Elijah the prophet demonstrated the power of God in a huge way, he had his world rocked when Ahab and Jezebel wanted to kill him. He ran away and hid under a tree by himself. He told the Lord, "Kill me, God." This is what happens when you are in trouble and you go off by yourself. A lack of perspective, stability and support can mess with your right mind when you get by yourself, away from God and the church.

My wife Lori had a very traumatizing experience happen when she was 19 years old. She and her family had packed up their car and were going to go on a vacation following church one Sunday morning. Her father was a pastor, and she and her brothers were sitting in the front row watching him preach. Suddenly, he died in the pulpit of a heart attack. Lori and her brothers all watched as their father died right in front of them while performing one of the routine acts of full time ministry. Now, years later, Lori and both of her brothers are in full time ministry. How could they all stay open to a God who would allow that to happen? It wasn't always that easy. Lori had a time where she was emotionless.

> I remember looking in the mirror and just smiling with my mouth and not my eyes. I couldn't eat and I felt lost. I felt numb. I remember being out with a friend of mine one night in college and seeing so many people and they were getting full on the world. I saw them become intoxicated and I thought about all of the times I experienced the presence of God in such a profound way in youth camps when I was growing up. I turned to my friend I was with and I told her it was all so empty. I couldn't fill myself like that. There was a time where I knew God so strongly and I couldn't go back to a place like a bar because I knew that I wanted to feel the strong presence of God again. I had hope for it again.
>
> I thought, "I am going to show up at church from now on." I just decided to pray

and read the Word just like I had when I could feel it. I did it all by faith even though I had no sense of feeling. It took several months to get to where I could even feel like I wanted to worship. I went to this church one night and I ended up sobbing to this elder in the church, just fell in a heap and cried. I told him that I was the daughter of a pastor and that I hadn't laughed or cried or experienced emotion in a long, long time. In that moment, everything negative was lifted from my life. The spirit of heaviness and depression was gone. I felt again and could laugh again. I still missed my dad, but the joy of the Lord in my life was restored.

The elder who prayed for her happened to own the home I was living in while in college. He would come home and tell me about this girl and what she had been through and the calling on her life. Months later Lori and I met and figured out that we both knew this man and that it was Lori that he was telling the story about.

Lori had an incredibly painful experience. Talk about having your world rocked. She was suddenly on her own. Before her father died, she knew that she wanted to be in ministry. After he died, she thought that dream had slipped away. She didn't know how she would ever be in ministry again. After months of struggling, she made a choice. She didn't leave the presence of God, she didn't allow herself to be alone, she pressed through even when she didn't feel like it. God met her right where she was. All in one night, hope started to take control again.

CHAPTER THREE

FIVE TRUTHS FOR THE PAIN

*M*aking the right choices in the wake of a painful situation is crucial. You can't make the right choices if you don't have the right information available to you. Many times we make wrong choices just because we aren't oriented around right beliefs. In this chapter we'll cover five core truths about your needs that will steer you correctly when you're disoriented by a world that's been rocked.

1. You need the presence of God.

You and I cannot stay away from Christ. He is our greatest need, and you will not make it through without

Him. As we learned before, the first thing Job did when it all came down was worship. Whether this means putting in a CD and singing or just being silent listening for God, commit to a daily devotion. Just open up your Bible and say, "Okay, Lord, talk to me." You need more than anything to worship through your pain.

Turn to the Psalms. There are all kinds of declarations of pain in that book, and they are all worship songs. Pick a place in your Bible and start reading. Make an effort with whatever strength you have. You'll begin to draw strength through those simple acts of worship, through songs, by just bowing your knee. I know it's tough and when you're weary, it's hard to know where to begin, but you must fight against closing yourself off from God. There are days I roll out of bed and I'll just sit on the side of the mattress and I have no idea what to say. You know, it's early in the morning. You haven't brushed your teeth. You're muttering, "I'm sorry, Lord. I'm just not awake yet." But if I just get on my knees and say to God, "I humble myself in your presence," God begins to work right there. That's worship: humbling yourself before God, being open to him.

Know that you need God. Choose to talk to him. Say, "I'm going to draw in to you, God." The Bible says, "Come near to God and he will come near to you" (James 4:8a). He's not going to leave you hanging.

Staying open and not clamming up is key in any relationship. When Jesus walked the earth, He was perfect, yet He took our sins. He stayed open to our needs. God is open to us no matter how many times we fail. This open love from Him can be enough to draw you into His presence.

2. You need to be in God's house.

Not only do you need to be in God's presence, you have to get into His presence in His house. You need God's house. I need God's house. We all need God's house. Do you know that just the simple act of getting dressed for church brings a discipline, an order, to your life that actually can be a comfort in a time of pain? Just knowing that you're going to church can be so good for you.

Don't put a wall between you, as Elijah did, and people whom God had set aside for your support. Later on, when Elijah hid himself in a cave, he told the Lord that he felt that he was the only one who was still serving the Lord. God told Him that there were 7,000 others who still pursued God along with Elijah (1 Kings 19). We often get lost in our little caves and never meet the 7,000 who could help us. The Bible talks about the church being set up on Mount Zion. I think it's because it's hard to get up a hill. God doesn't put the church down, setting it low in a valley. He sets the church up, which means you've got to have some discipline in your life to get there, and you have to make some decisions in your life to make getting there part of your regular routine. I know it's not always easy. When your world is rocked, sometimes you don't even want to get out of bed, much less leave your house. You have to because whether you will admit it or not, you need the presence of others.

In Genesis, a man named Cain became jealous of his brother Abel and killed him. God asked Cain where his brother was because he was missing. Cain replied flippantly, "Am I my brother's keeper?" When Cain said he wasn't his brother's keeper, was he telling the truth? God's questioning here showed that Cain was actually partly accountable for Abel's well being. When God put all those "one another's" in the New Testament, He was not just blowing smoke. All of these words are in Scripture because we are our brother's keeper, and we are supposed to live in a sort of "one another" mentality.

The reality is that when you and I find ourselves rocked, we need one another. God has designed our world to run on the system of community. Jesus says, "For where two or three come together in my name, there am I with them" (Matthew 18:20). God *will* also meet with you in the secret place. It's okay sometimes to close the door and get alone, just you and God, but God also says, "I am not going to answer you in all the ways that I need to answer you and you're not going to say all the things you need to say to Me, unless you get together with others." This is why He set up the need for the church and Christian community.

Hebrews 10:19-25 says:

> Therefore, brothers, since we have confidence to enter the Most Holy Place by the blood of Jesus, by a new and living way opened for us through the curtain, that is, His body, and since we have a great priest over the house of God, let us draw near to God with a sincere heart in full assurance of faith, having our hearts sprinkled to cleanse us from a guilty conscience and having our bodies washed with pure water. Let us hold unswervingly to

the hope we profess, for He who promised is faithful. And let us consider how we may spur one another on toward love and good deeds. Let us not give up meeting together, as some are in the habit of doing, but let us encourage one another—and all the more as you see the Day approaching.

Notice that these verses say the opposite of "giving up." The gathering with the church is "encouraging one another." Encouragement is what happens when you come to church; it's one of the main reasons the church exists. You start exhorting one another. This is what I'm doing right now. I'm encouraging you. I'm like the coach on the sidelines shouting instructions and cheering you on, "Let's go! You can do it!"

This passage from Hebrews says to do all this stuff "all the more as you see the Day approaching." Which day? The great day of the Lord. The day when this whole world will be fully and totally rocked. We can't slack off. We can't neglect worship, we can't neglect gathering together. We have to keep up our intensity.

This is why I think in some respects rocked worlds are good for church growth: people suddenly realize they need God to help them. Where do you go when you're in financial ruin, relational ruin, marital ruin, emotional ruin, and you don't know where to turn? Some people get desperate and will give God a try. Some people were religious at one time and they want to turn to God. Where do they go to hear from God? Right after 9/11, there was a spike in church attendance. America was rocked. Suddenly there were a lot of searchers wanting to get their priorities right.

You need to stay in church when your world is rocked. The key is that everything that can be shaken will be shaken. Jesus declared to Peter that the kingdom of Hell will not prevail against His church. His church will not be shaken. When the shaking happens, the best and only place to be is with His church.

3. You need the right people.

The "right people." I would love to have written "God's people." It is important to be with God's people, but I'm not saying "God's people" in this instance, because sometimes God's people say some really stupid things.

My son Jackson had a painful boil on his shoulder. Now, I don't think my 8 year old, when he got a boil on his shoulder, is Job (even though Job suffered from boils).

I didn't say to Jackson, "You know, son, let me just tell you something – there is sin in your life. You're 8, but you've got some issues. God is striking you with boils. Being in a pastor's family entails a stricter judgment. So be encouraged, son. It could be worse, and it probably will be." That's the sort of stupidity Job's friends dumped on him. They urged him to find a "why" in his suffering that didn't really exist. They couldn't comprehend the surprise of suffering. From their perspective, somehow Job must have earned his trouble.

There are some people that might not even be saved, yet they know how to say the right thing to you in your moment of need. Meanwhile, there are some Christians who can say some really unhelpful things, even though they don't mean to. In the midst of a tragic loss, some may say, "Well, God just loved them so much he had to take them." Or, "God needed another angel, and that's why he took your baby." Some of these statements are not helpful, some are hurtful, and some are not even doctrinal. God does not take people and turn them into angels. He creates people to be people, and he creates angels to be angels. You don't become an angel after you die.

These things (and lots of others) that Christians sometimes say can not only be unhelpful, they can be hurtful. When someone adds the additional burden of bad doctrine or uncomforting comfort, it can make your pain heavier.

When my world is rocked, I want the right people around me. Many times it is God's people who say the right things, but sometimes it's not God's people who say the right things. That's when you pray, "Lord, give me the right people. Give me some people that have some wisdom." You need wise counsel, wherever you can find it.

4. You need to stay positive.

Do you remember what Job said as he was worshiping in the presence of the Lord? He says:

> Naked I came from my mother's womb,
> and naked I will depart.
> The LORD gave and the LORD
> has taken away;
> may the name of the LORD be praised.
> (Job 1:21)

I think what Job is expressing is an attitude that says, "God, I just lost my camel dealership. I lost my sheep dealership. I lost my oxen. I've lost it. I've lost my livelihood. I've lost my profession. I've lost my place. I'm losing my house. I'm going to lose it all. I don't have that country club anymore. I can't pay the bills." And then on top of that, he's lost his family. Job is acknowledging in positive prayer, "Lord, everything came from you. It's not mine. None of it is. Those kids that I had the privilege of raising, God, thank you, but they ultimately belong to you."

It's a radical trust to acknowledge our place like that. It takes a powerful positivity to see tragedy from that perspective.

I think Job is showing an attitude of gratefulness. I think at the end of this Scripture, when he says "may the name of the LORD be praised," he is making a determined commitment to say, I'm going to bless you, Lord, through all of this. And I am going to be positive. I am not going to be negative. And I'm not going to let vinegar come out of my mouth. I am not going to let myself come out on the other side of this as a bitter person.

Looking ahead, we will cover Job's restoration. He received twice as much at the end of his life as he had at the beginning of his life. This is why the Bible will go on to tell us in James 5:11 to consider the perseverance of Job, to ponder how he ended up. It doesn't tell us to dwell on the beginning or the middle of his story, but to consider his perseverance, to dwell on the end of the story. When it's all said and done, Job's life is back up on top again. Why? Because he refused to go negative.

The Apostle Paul says when you're going through trouble and your world is being rocked, *"Rejoice in the Lord always. I will say it again: Rejoice!"* (Philippians 4:4). He says it twice! Many times we don't want to rejoice the first time. In fact, I think he says it twice to remind us to be determined to rejoice, to make a concentrated effort to be positive. I've got to *make* myself rejoice. That's why Paul says "Rejoice!" twice. And it's why David says this: "Bless the LORD, O my soul, and all that is within me" (Psalm 103:1 ESV). He's commanding his soul to praise God. He's not just saying something. He's concentrated on "all that is within" himself and commanding it to bless God. David singles out his own soul and tells it to bless God. It's like an out of body experience. He's focusing his inner being on God, he is making a determination to be worshipful. He's going positive, not negative.

Why do we invest so much time in earthly treasures that will come back to nothing? Why do we treat temporary things like they're permanent? Why do we treat anything like it's ours and not God's? The answer to all these questions is why Job says, "May the name of the LORD be praised." He had a flood of negative things happening to him, but he could be eternally positive because he knew his relationship with God could never be taken away.

If your world is crumbling all around you, make a determination to praise the name of the Lord. You have this confidence and assurance that your relationship with Christ is secure and He will never leave you or forsake you in your trial or pain.

5. You need to move forward.

Your positive attitude needs to project you in a positive direction. "In all this," notice what the Bible says, "Job did not sin by charging God with wrongdoing" (Job 1:22). Think about this for a second. What happens when we are in the mess of pain and suffering and grief? We tend to be negative and then start to retreat. We hunker down, we get alone, and we build up walls. We stew. We wallow. Ever heard of a pity party? We can throw some good ones.

We sit in one place and pity ourselves while we blame everybody else. When we do that, we stagnate spiritually.

The Bible says that in all that was happening to him, Job determined he was not going to go backwards. He fell down before God in worship, but he refused to fall back into sinful habits and patterns and playing the blame-game. He moved forward.

Most people, when they find their worlds rocked, instead of maintaining a spiritually upright position, they end up giving up ground to the enemy and allowing themselves to go back to things they've been delivered from. Instead of maintaining and holding that ground, they end up going back to drinking, drugs, or pornography. They feel weak and they indulge their flesh rather than standing on the Word of God. Rocked and stagnant people retreat back to that vice, that habit, that bad attitude that God had set them free from. And they allow some things to come back into their life, thinking it's going to comfort them, thinking they deserve it, thinking it's going to help them. Job, I believe, said "I'm not going to sin. I'm not going backwards." He refused to backslide under the weight of the ruins of his life. He moved forward.

Years ago, I was pastoring a man who was doing really well in our church. He was growing quickly in the Lord. And he started a business. All of a sudden, like it happened to Job, everything came down. The business collapsed. Do you know what he told me one day? He said, "Pastor Joe, based on what I've been through, I deserve to smoke a joint."

What this guy had in his mind is what surfaces in our own minds when the world around us crumbles: I deserve relief, a drink, a smoke. I deserve it. This backward *spirit of entitlement* is what leads men and women to cheat on their spouses: they think they deserve someone else. Their marriage is crumbling, and they think, "I deserve to have this affair." They think, "I'm just not getting what I need." Then their needs become the center of their universe. They end up allowing the devil to get a foothold in their lives that will eventually become a stronghold. So in seeking relief, people end up worse.

The Bible says Job didn't go backwards into sinful habits or blaming God and arguing about what he thought he deserved.

All of this sounds great but moving forward may seem too difficult. Maybe it takes all you've got just to keep from moving backwards. Sometimes that's okay. There are seasons of suffering where you can't move forward but by God's strength you can at least stand. You're not pursuing, maybe, but you're not retreating either. I think this is why the Bible says in Ephesians 6:11, when you've done all you can, "take your stand against the devil's schemes." Just stand. In verse 14 it says "stand firm." Sometimes it's not about moving forward. Sometimes it's just about holding your ground. Gather up all you've got within you in worship and positivity and faith, and refuse to be moved. Just stand still and let the storm pass. Don't give up. Sometimes just weathering the storm is the progress God requires of you.

While you're taking your stand, however, remember that even as you are expressing how you feel about the storm of life, don't accuse God. Accusing God is going backwards too, even if you're standing upright. Don't shake your fist at God. Think about all that Job lost, and the fact that we know from the first chapter of his story that God allowed this stuff to happen. God wasn't ignorant of it. God wasn't powerless to prevent it from happening. He let it happen. Yet Job brought no charge against God. He did not accuse God of being evil, wicked, or cruel.

It takes taking a stand in faith to trust God when your world is rocked. Standing your ground means blessing God, loving Him, committing to worship Him, determining in your soul to be positive toward God. Why? It's probably one of the most powerful truths that you can find as it relates to what God is doing when we're in our time of suffering, when we're being afflicted. Isaiah 63:9 tells us this: "In all their distress He too was distressed." I love this scripture. This is so powerful. God says about you and me, in all our afflictions, He—God Himself—is afflicted. In other words, when you're hurting, God's hurting.

Where do you think it comes from that, after we rushed my son Jackson to the emergency room, while they were lancing his infected boil, and I'm trying to hold him still and trying to keep him from looking, my wife Lori is hunched over, in agony herself, crying, devastated? Where does that come from? She felt the pain along with Jackson. That identification with the pain of her son, the identification that I had with Jackson in that pain—do you think that comes from chance? No, that comes from a Father who loves his children, a Father who put that connection in all of us because it's in Him too.

While Lori and I were feeling what Jackson was going through, I got a text from his 16 and 11 year old brothers asking, "Can we get ice cream? How's Jackson?" Talk about priorities in need of straightening! I said to them, "Right now Jackson is being cut on. He's withering in pain as they stuffed gauze in his wound. Can we please identify with Jackson right now and identify with his pain? So there will be no ice cream until Jackson can eat and drink again." They texted me back: "Good idea. You're right, but let us know as soon as Jackson can eat and drink again." They wanted to know when they could get ice cream.

Here's what I want to say to you: when you're hurting, God is not thinking about ice cream. He's thinking about *you*. When you're hurting, He's hurting with you. He hurts with you right now. If you're troubled, He feels your pain. In your affliction, He's afflicted. He cares about you.

I would love to be able to say we have an answer to all of the "why?" questions, but we don't. We live in a fallen world. That's why God sent his Son in the first place. Why do people suffer? There's a fallen world, and it has fallen because of sin. But God has said, "I sent my boy, my only son, to heal you and to deliver you and to set you free." There is something special and powerful about the presence of God that manifests when you're hurting. Job knew this. He's basically saying, "I am going to express my complaint, but I am also going to worship God and I am going to get in to the presence of God and I'm going to get in to the presence of people, and I am going to bless the Lord and I am not going to sin and I'm not going to go backwards. I'm going to trust God."

Jesus knew He was going to have to undergo some terrible things and then die. He knew His disciples were going to end up living under persecution and go to their own deaths. He promises them this will happen and He warns them. But He says this to them: "Do not let your hearts be troubled. Trust in God; trust also in Me" (John 14:1). Then He said to them:

> In my Father's house are many rooms; if it were not so, I would have told you. I am going there to prepare a place for you. And if I go and prepare a place for you, I will come back and take you to be with me that you also may be where I am. You know the way to the place where I am going.
>
> (John 14:2-4)

The first thing Thomas could think to say was, "Lord, we don't know where you are going, so how can we know the way?" (John 14:5) Jesus said to Him, "I am the way and the truth and the life" (John 14:6).

Jesus knows our way is going to be marked by trouble and difficulty. He knows we're going to lose loved ones and lose loved things. He knows life isn't easy. Yet He's looking out for us. And He tells us the way to the Father is through Him!

We must walk through life focused more on the way of Jesus than the way of the world. We have to fix our eyes on Jesus while the walls crumble around us. Let's cling to the rock of our salvation when our world is rocked.

You have a choice to let your heart be troubled or not. Believe that God is in absolute control and that He is going to reward your faith.

CHAPTER FOUR

WHAT'S NEXT?

What do I mean when I say the word "rocked?" To be rocked means to be hit with a blow, to be punched, to be struck, and to not have an answer for any of it. You may not literally be struck with physical pain, but to have your world rocked sometimes means to feel as though a boulder has been dropped on you. If you've only ever experienced a life of relative calm and comfort, to all of a sudden experience being rocked can feel like being suffocated. It can leave you confused, speechless. At some point in your life, if you haven't already, you will have your world rocked. It *will* happen. It all comes down in a day.

It happened to Rex and Mona, members of Celebration Church, in January of 2000. Rex begins their story:

> We have four daughters: Meghan, who is seventeen, and Abigail who is fourteen, and we have Laura who is ten, and Morgan who is seven. The girls were very excited that it had snowed. The snow was beautiful that morning, and it was quite a lot of snow for Indiana.
>
> That afternoon, after getting home and getting all bundled up, we set out to join a couple of neighborhood kids in the local neighborhood that had a sledding hill. They took off. And of course the joy of just getting to watch them, as a dad anyway, was awesome. And then I saw the truck coming just about the time the kids got down to the bottom of the hill. And it was very, very hard to see and to comprehend. I knew both the girls had gotten down there. And the truck had hit them. Meghan was actually in the front of the truck, and from what I could tell, it ran over her.
>
> Pretty much everything just stopped, moved in slow motion. It was very hard to describe or even understand what was happening. I thought they would just get up and that the truck had just missed them. But that wasn't the case. And Meghan laid there. Her head was deformed. It had actually run over her head. And I just cried out. I yelled. I don't know what I yelled, but the realization I had was I knew my daughter wasn't with us anymore. And Abby was crying about 20 feet

away. And I just had a sense of taking care of what I could.

The girls' mother Mona continues:

> When I got there, I saw the girls laying in the street, and I just knew. My heart just sank. I went over near Meghan; she was laying just lifeless. And my body just crumpled on the ground. I felt like I could just melt in to the snow. That's how you feel. You just don't know what to do. You're just so shocked.

Rex adds:

> There's somewhat of a feeling right away that I knew she wasn't with us anymore. And I didn't know why. I didn't understand why. I knew there was nothing I could do, although they tried to revive her and do several things. The scene was horrific. The way you look at TV, the way you look at music, the way you look at individuals, it was totally rocked, totally changed, totally undeterminable. Nothing was the same.
>
> Through a tragedy, we found out that for us it magnified who we already were. Setting those priorities early made all the difference in the world with dealing with something that our minds couldn't comprehend. What God has shown me and developed in me has been an appreciation for heaven more than I had before. I knew Jesus. I looked forward to

seeing Him one day when I go to heaven. But now all of a sudden I have flesh in heaven.

My daughter is in heaven. And I felt guilty about that at first. I thought, "I want to go to heaven to see my daughter." But God taught me, "Rex, now you get it. You get it. That's how I felt when my son was on earth and I brought Him to me. Now, you understand what true love is, what a father's love is." Yeah, I desire to see her, but God says now you need to show that to other people. You need to see and help them understand what God's love is on earth before it's your time to come home to see your daughter.

Mona concludes:

I felt like everything I had known or had thought about until then was just peeled away until there was, you know, just my faith and trust. What are you going to do from here, you know? And I had to slowly build up that stuff, you know? Over time, day after day, moment by moment, know that God is building a solid foundation.

Have you heard of "joy unspeakable"? Well, Rex and Mona are describing a pain that is very near unspeakable. For many of us, talking about having our lives fall apart is not some flippant means of explaining an inconvenience.

It is about losing what is most precious to us in the worst ways imaginable.

This is what happened to Job.

Job personifies, in the realest way possible, a world that is rocked. In a couple of days, a matter of minutes, Job's very world crumbled around him. His financial world was rocked, of course, because the business he'd built by his own blood and sweat vanished in the storm. But his world really came crashing down when he lost his children. The loss of his business was insult; but the loss of his children—his sons and his daughters—was injury.

It's one thing to lose your business and to lose your finances and to lose your fiscal security, but it's another thing entirely to lose your children. Added to that, Job began to lose his body. Boils began to break out on his body (Job 2:7). He was rapidly losing his health. The destruction of his world moved from his business to his children to his body. Everything in Job's life was rocked. Anything that could be broken or killed *was*. And I think it's interesting that the book of Job is the oldest biblical manuscript we have. It's the oldest book in the Bible. Most scholars believe it was written before Genesis. It is almost as if God is saying, "Everybody's world is going to be rocked, and that's why I'm starting with Job. I want you to be prepared."

You may know what it's like to lose a child. Or maybe you know what it's like to lose a child to sin; though they're not dead, in their prodigal ways they may feel as though they are. When your world is rocked deeply like this, shaking your very foundation, something happens. You want to know why. You begin to ask the perennial question: "Why, God?" You want to know what's happening.

That's the common question, and it's an almost instinctual reaction to the pain we're experiencing, but there's another question that actually runs deeper than "why." It's a question that Job asked. It's a question that we all want to know when we have lost something. When Rex and Mona lost their daughter that day, they lost not just their child, but also all the dreams they had for her, all their plans, the entire future they saw with her in it. They weren't anticipating a future without Meghan in it, so when she was taken so suddenly, so terribly, so was their future. Their confusion gave birth to another question, the one deeper than "why."

My wife's dad, Bill, died at the age of 45 while he was preaching. He had three young kids, my wife the oldest.

Bill used to talk to the kids all the time about one day all of them living on the same street. Their plan was to be all together. "We're all going to live on Elmwood Parkway," he'd say. He'd say to Lori, "This is where you're going to live. You're going to buy that lot. Because I'll build a house *here*." And then he'd turn to her brother, "Now you guys are gonna live right here . . ." When Bill died, that dream died. The life he'd built up, with all its hopes and goals, died along with him.

When your world is rocked, your dreams die. When someone close to you dies, something inside of you dies. You end up grieving more than just the loss of your loved one. And it makes you ask a question, the *right* question. It's a question that I believe we all want answered, every one of us. It's a question connected to creation itself.

Will a Man Live Again?

Look what Job says in Job 14:14: "If a man dies, will he live again?"

"God, I want to know something," he's saying. "Can I live again after my world has been rocked?"

Can you live again after your world has crashed, after you have experienced the pain of death? You probably know the answer, but you're going to ask the question anyway when trouble comes.

The answer to the question is *yes*. The truth is, you *can* live again.

Meghan's mother Mona is asking, "Can we trust again? Can we believe God again? Can we feel again?" Well, can we? Can we have that confidence again? Can we take family vacations again? Do we have the right? Rex felt guilty about saying he wanted to see his daughter again. Can he feel okay about that?

When Lazarus died, his sisters were shaken to the core. Martha and Mary were beside themselves with grief. They'd lost their brother, whom they loved deeply. But Jesus offers some perspective: "Did I not tell you," he said, "that if you believed you would see the glory of God?" After remembering this story, he heard God saying, "Rex, you get it." Because that's what God sent Jesus to do: restore you and put into your life the ability and the power, through his own death and resurrection, to truly live again.

The phrase "I'll believe it when I see it" is not the way faith works. Jesus says you'll see it *after* you believe it. This is the key to trusting that after your world is rocked, you can live again.

Five Ways to Live Again

By God's power working through your faith, there are ways that "a man can live again." In Job 14:14, he asks the core question: "If a man dies, will he live again?" And then he declares:

> All the days of my hard service
> I will wait for my renewal to come.
> You will call and I will answer you.
> (Job 14:14-15a)

Job's determination is to wait for God to show up, and to be ready when He does. This tells us the first way you can live again after your world is rocked.

1. You can live again if you don't quit in the day of battle.

Right after Job asks, "Lord, can I live?" he says, "I am going to handle this struggle." He knows he's going to struggle through his days of pain. When your world is rocked, there is a period of time of real struggle. The world can come crashing down all in one day, but the wake of pain and suffering and grief it brings can last days. Or weeks. Or months. Maybe even years. When you are processing the news, you're going to have to learn how to fight. Job determines, "I am going to struggle through this, God."

I'm always nervous when I go to a funeral for a young child and I meet with the family. Have you ever heard of an "untimely death"? There's really no such thing as a "timely death," I guess, but when a child dies, that's the epitome of an untimely death. It's not right when a parent outlives his or her child. I know that there are times where parents mourning a loss like this are carried through a season supernaturally by the Spirit, but I do become a little nervous when a grieving family says, "Pastor, I just know God is on the throne." I think, "Praise God," but I get a little nervous because I don't know if they're really processing the struggle. I want to say hallelujah right along with them, but I worry it's not real, that they may actually be doing more harm than good by not allowing themselves to feel their pain and work through the struggle of grief. This is why the Bible says to mourn with those who mourn—because there is a time to weep, a time for mourning (Romans 12:15; Ecclesiastes 3:4). Weeping is made for rocked worlds. It's okay to say, "I'm struggling with this."

Job knew the key to handling the struggle was not quitting when he was in the midst of that struggle. I was told once by one of the men in our church that his wife suddenly said, "I'm filing for divorce this week. It's over." Thirteen years of marriage, gone. He was processing. He was struggling. He was asking the why questions to his wife and to God. I told him the key to persevering, to finding life out of the sudden train wreck of divorce, lay in how he was going to handle the struggle. You've got to keep going, keep loving, keep trusting. Don't quit. Jesus himself was struggling with the world-rocking promise of the cross. He said, "Lord, I don't want to go through this struggle, and if there is any way possible that you can deliver me from this situation, then do it" (Luke 22:42). But in total awareness of the weight of his fear and anxiety, he also said, "Lord, I am going to stay committed even through this struggle. Not my will but yours be done."

You too will live again if you don't quit in the day of battle.

In Hebrews 12:3-4, notice what it says to do: *consider Jesus*. Whenever you find yourself in a struggle consider—or think about—Jesus. Consider the one "who endured such opposition." Why? Hebrews 12:3 says "so that you will not grow weary and lose heart." Ephesians 6:10 tells us that when we're in the battle to "be strong in the Lord and in His mighty power." Notice it says "in *His* mighty power," not yours. That whole passage in Ephesians 6 is about the need to put on the armor of God to withstand outside attacks. In other words, you'd better get your hands on every piece of spiritual equipment you can so that you will be able to stand firm against the strategy of the devil. His strategy is to take you out in your battle, to crush you when you're struggling. Our tendency is to stop fighting. The tendency is to give up. We give ourselves to other things. Instead of giving ourselves to the Lord, we give ourselves to alcohol. We give ourselves to drugs. We give ourselves to pornography. We give ourselves to infidelity. We give up the fight and we give ourselves to things we think will bring satisfaction in other ways, because we're just tired.

Moses got tired in the day of struggle. The Israelites were fighting a battle and the Lord told Moses to keep his arms in the air. As long as they were in the air, the Israelites won the battle. His hands got heavy and he wanted to bring them down (Exodus 17:8-16). And God said, "Moses, you've got to stay in the fight. You've got to stay in the struggle. Get your hands back up." In fact, God brought people around Moses to get his hands back up. And when his hands went up, guess what? The struggle began to turn in the Israelites' favor. When his hands went down, the enemy began to take ground. I just have to tell you, "Put your hands back up." If you don't quit, the battle is the Lord's. He's going to see you through your rocked world.

If a man dies, will he live again? Yes. If he doesn't quit.

2. You can live again if you remain patient.

In Job 14:14, Job basically says, "Lord, in these days of struggle, I'm going to wait." Despite all that is going on in his life, despite all the loss he has suffered, despite the uncertainty that losing everything suddenly creates, Job remains committed. Patience is commitment. It is a commitment to the ways of God.

Rex and Mona could very easily have said, "This whole Christianity thing, this whole Jesus thing, this whole God protecting us thing didn't work." They could have chucked it all. But they didn't. Why? How could they keep trusting, keep waiting on God?

When the pain is deep, you have to go deep. You've got to reach way down and cling to your core commitments, trusting that God is doing something powerful, even if you can't see it yet, in your pain. In these moments is when you begin to say, with resolve, "God, I know you are true." This is exactly what Jesus did in His moment of fear and anxiety before the cross. Facing the alternatives to God's painful plan, He decided to wait it out. He says to the Father, "I'm going to stay committed to Your plan. I'm going to stay committed to Your purpose. I'm going to stay committed to who You are, God."

When you are facing the most difficult battles of your life, when you are wondering how on earth you will ever be able to go on living, you are going to have to learn how to stay committed. You *will* live again if you will have the patience enough to outlast your struggle.

James 5:7 says, "Be patient, then, brothers, until the Lord's coming." James connects this patience to that of a farmer waiting for his land to yield its crops. Just as the farmer has to work hard and wait for the good stuff, we have to be patient for the fruit of whatever God is sowing in our lives when our world is rocked. You will wait through sun and rain. You will wait through calm days and days when the wind is beating against you. You will wait through days you can't see any growth at all. But you wait and you trust. And you wait some more. You "be patient and stand firm," James 5:8 says. Why? "Because the Lord's coming is near." He is going to come near to you.

When our world is rocked, we say, "God, where are You?" But He is right there, and He's drawing nearer and nearer, even if you can't feel Him through your pain. Be patient. Wait on Him. Wait for the return of the feeling of His presence. Trust it's going to come.

James goes on to say in verse 9 that when we don't do this, we end up complaining. We complain against God and then we end up complaining against others. Our impatience with God leads to impatience with others. Our anger over the process of pain and grief leads us to grumble against people. We end up turning against each other. James says not to do that. Our God sees how we're responding to our pain and grief. He knows if we are waiting patiently, fighting for our faith, or if we're grumbling impatiently and fighting others.

When you are processing the rubble of a rocked world, let the Lord be the judge of your life. Don't move in to false judgments of your situation or of others. Don't surrender to fatalistic negativity. Stay committed, stay patient. James goes on to say:

> Brothers, as an example of patience in the face of suffering, take the prophets who spoke in the name of the Lord. As you know, we consider blessed those who have persevered. You have heard of Job's perseverance and have seen what the Lord finally brought about. The Lord is full of compassion and mercy.
> (James 5:10-11)

The prophets persevered. They were patient even in the "face of suffering." They stayed committed to God. "Do you remember Job?" James asks. "Do you remember his perseverance?" What sort of crop did his patience yield? Job would end up with twice as much at the end of his life as he had at the beginning. He had more at the end! God is full of compassion and mercy, and Job was patient enough to see that.

You will live again after your world is rocked if you don't quit and if you stay patient, but there's a third way as well:

3. You can live again if you embrace change.

"I will wait," Job says, "for my renewal to come" (Job 14:14). He saw that as good and successful as he was—and the story tells us that he was blameless and upright, and that he was an extremely successful and wealthy man—there were still some changes that God wanted to make in his life. What Job came to understand is that through his situation—through losing his business, his children, and now his body—he realized that God was going to bring him to a whole new level. He realized that it takes ending one level to go to another level, and that God wanted to actually advance him and bring him further than he could have ever gotten on his own. God wanted to move him from being good to being great. God wanted to bring him in to a greater experience of God himself. He wanted to bring him in to a greater experience of worship.

When your world is rocked, if you want to know if you can live again, God *will* be urging you to change. He *will* be asking you in your pain to embrace whatever change is necessary to prevail. This is a whole new aspect of the challenge of processing pain, because we oftentimes don't want to let go. We don't want to change. We want to keep everything the same. When we're grieving, as we're thinking back to how things were, we start to wish we could go back in time. The way out is the way forward, to whatever lies ahead. You can't go back anyway. It's not possible. God says to you that you can't live if you won't let go. Jesus says, "Whoever loses his life for my sake will find it" (Matthew 10:39).

In John 11, He says to Martha and Mary, "I know you're rocked. I know your faith is shaken. I know your trust in me is tested. I know you love your brother Lazarus. But you know I love him too. I know it's messing up your world that I didn't show up. I know it's messing up your world he's been dead for four days. I know you just told me to forget it, that it's too late. But I'm telling you right now that if you believe and that if you will let me have my way in your life, what looks bad right now will turn out for a change for the better." And he raised Lazarus from the dead.

Here's what Job says:

> I know that you can do all things;
> no plan of yours can be thwarted.
> You asked, "Who is this that obscures my
> counsel without knowledge?"
> Surely I spoke of things I did not
> understand,
> things too wonderful for me to know.

You said, "Listen now, and I will speak;
I will question you,
and you shall answer me."
My ears had heard of you
but now my eyes have seen you.
(Job 42:2-5)

Job *thought* he knew God. Then he experienced this rocked world. He didn't know God like he could have known God, because it took this experience to bring him in to another level of faith. In the first couple of verses of Job 42, we see that Job has his theology straightened out: "I know your plans can't be thwarted," he says. He knows God is all-powerful. He has that head knowledge. But in verse 5 he's admitting that his belief was based only on having heard those truths. In trusting God after his world has been rocked, he now *sees* those truths. Do you know what Job was declaring? "I thought I knew you until I had this experience," he's saying to God. All along he was doing what he was told to do. He prayed, he worked, he worshiped, he lived, he trusted. He did all the right stuff. But Job had a level of life with God that still had room for more. And this is the gist of Job's confession in chapter 42: "I used to do what I did by the head, but now I do it from the heart." His own eyes had a hold of God's truth!

Job realized that his life was rocked from top to bottom because God wanted to bring a change in his life from top to bottom.

When you start changing, you'll start living. Sometimes God allows your world to be rocked because the massive changes required in processing that pain is the beginning of massive growth in your life. You will figure out how to live again when you figure out how to embrace change.

4. You can live again if you obey.

As Job is quoting God, he's saying, "Lord, when you call, I am going to answer" (Job 42:4). When God talks, Job is going to listen. When God commands, Job is going to obey. Here's what I want you to hear: Job is simply saying he doesn't want to stay in this place of death. He wants out. He wants to see some fruit from his fight and his patience. So he says, "When you call, God, I am going to be more sensitive to your voice." In our opening story, recall Rex saying everything became different. The way he watched television, the way he lived, the way he spent money, the way conversations sounded, the way the world looked—it all changes.

What changes more than anything else is your *ear*. Your ear changes. When your world is rocked you are more attentive than ever to whatever God will say to you, aren't you? Jesus says, "If you love me, you will obey what I command" (John 14:15). Job shows us the way to get life again when our world has been rocked: "I am going to answer you, God, like I've never answered you before. I'm going to answer you when you call." In our pain, God is calling. He is speaking to us in our pain. We will find our life again if in response to His call we will be sensitive, attentive, and say, "Here I am, Lord. Send me."

Ask God, "What are you calling forth out of my life?" Ask Him. He is placing a call upon your life. And when your world is rocked, He's equipping you to hear it, because He knows you're going to feel your need for Him most when your supports and your successes have been taken away.

You will live again after a rocked world if you don't quit, if you remain patient, if you embrace change, and if you obey God.

5. You can live again if you have a vision.

When Job says he is waiting for the renewal to come, he is realizing that God has a vision for him that has not been fulfilled (Job 14:14). God wants that vision to be complete. Even though Job had lost his business, even though he had lost his children, and even though he had lost health in his body, he recognized that there was still a work for God to do in his life.

I want to challenge you with this: There is a vision to be fulfilled in your life. The only way that you are going to get out of this world of yours that has been rocked is to begin to fight for your future. When my wife Lori was diagnosed with cancer, she was 23 years old and 7 months pregnant. We weren't even sure if Lori was going to live, much less the baby. But a word came to us, and here's what it said: "You're going to see your grandchildren, Lori." Suddenly our perspective changed. It changed from fighting for today to fighting for the future. As Paul told Timothy to fight according to the prophecy that was given to him when the presbytery laid their hands on him (1 Timothy 1:18), we clung to God's vision for us in our battle for our future.

God's vision to give you a future and a hope is there for your claiming (Jeremiah 29:11). You will live if you fight for your future. "Where there is no vision, the people perish" (Proverbs 29:18 KJV). But when there is a vision, there is hope for the future.

CHAPTER FIVE

BATTLING BETRAYAL

*W*hen your world is rocked, you will be tempted to think all hope is lost. You will be tempted to think life is over. You will face a future you can't see, a future you can't believe in. The difference between someone who is overcome with despair and someone who overcomes despair with perseverance is fighting for that unseen future.

Fighting for your future is difficult when all you see is the glory of your past and the rubble of your present. All your hope may have been placed in things that don't exist anymore. Now more than ever you have to trust in the invisible God, believing that He will grant you visible comfort again. The comfort of your past may betray you. You might have long rested in your successes and accomplishments. You may have actually let love for your family replace your love for God. Maybe your family became your god. You will find whether this is true or not if your family is taken from you. Do you stay in the despair? Or do you gradually heal and still trust God?

Making the choices to get to that point of healing and trusting God is part of the answer to how you fight for the future you can't see.

What makes this fight even harder is when your support system turns on you. The world turns on you; then your friends and family turn on you.

This is what happened to Job. So in this chapter we're going to see what to do when you're not just fighting through the rocked world of loss of business, children, and bodily health, but what to do when you're also fighting through the rocked world of betrayal.

Lower than Low

Job couldn't go any lower. I mean, what else could he lose? He'd lost his businesses and his finances. He'd lost his children. He'd lost his health, as boils invaded his skin. How can it get worse? What else is there? Things had become so bad the Bible says Job actually cursed the day he was born (Job 3:1). He wished he was dead.

Have you ever been there? Millions of people commit suicide every year, and millions more at least ponder it. We don't know if Job was truly suicidal, but it would be understandable if he was, wouldn't it? He had been pressed so low, he was cursing the day he was born.

What you need to make sure in a time like this, as we've seen in a previous chapter, is that you do not stay alone. You can't enter solitude. You have to surround yourself with the right people.

Job didn't have the right people close by. He was looking for help, looking for encouragement. He had these friends: Eliphaz, Bildad, and Zophar. The Bible calls them Job's friends, anyway, and it says they came near to encourage him, but the result was anything but encouraging. They found Job in his lowest state and made it so that he sank even lower.

The Bitterness of Betrayal

While Job's friends are on their way to talk with him, I believe they have already formed an opinion and a conviction about why Job is in his situation. They come to the conclusion that Job must be in sin. "Job must be wrong," they think. "We have not really seen the real side of Job," they believe. And without seeing him, without talking with him, without sitting down and ministering to him, without praying with him, without hearing from him, they have already determined in their mind that Job has to have deserved what happened to him. They come to give advice, but it all hinges on Job being the cause of his own suffering.

In most of the book, Job is wrestling not with the loss of his business, not with the loss of his family, not with the loss of his physical health, but with how to handle betrayal. Most of us will have to deal with betrayal in our lives. If you're going to attempt anything significant in your life, you will have to deal with betrayal at some point.

Job has to deal with betrayal because his friends are just as confused as he is, and they use bad doctrine to work their way out of it. Things like this don't happen, they think, if you're living right, living clean, living well. You don't go from being at the top of the food chain to the bottom overnight unless there are some serious issues in your life. So where the Bible tells us Job was blameless and upright (Job 1:1), his friends are thinking, "Nah, couldn't be." They can't fathom a world where bad things happen to good people. In their world, only bad people have bad things happen to them. Job is looking for comfort; he's looking to be embraced. Instead he's betrayed.

Where his friends should have been standing with him and for him, when his friends should have been ministering to him, they're hurting him. The arm they're placing around his neck is really a knife in his back. They don't mean to, but they betray him.

Betrayal can be more damaging, more devastating, and more detrimental than any amount of lost finances or health. A lost loyalty can be a crushing defeat. This is why I really believe that battling through betrayal is more of a defining moment than any other single event in the life of a person. Why? Because betrayal comes through the hands of those whom we love, those whom we trusted, and those whom we involved our life with. Betrayal is traumatic because it rocks our relational world, and relationship is what we were designed for.

I once talked to a gentleman who said after almost 20 years of upper management employment with a company, they just simply said you're done. Out of the blue, he was fired after decades of loyal service. As a pastor, I hear many stories about the betrayal of abuse and its long held secret within families. When something like that comes to light it is incredibly traumatic, because the very people that were depended upon for support and survival turn out to violate us. The ones we love turn against us, they walk out on us, and they judge us.

Job puts some feeling behind his experience of betrayal.

> How long will you torment me
> and crush me with words?
> Ten times now you have reproached me;
> shamelessly you attack me.
> (Job 19:2-3)

Job wants to know when enough will be enough. "Haven't I been hurt enough?" he's asking. When will it stop? And he's talking not about the pain of what's happened to him but the pain of what his friends are saying to him! He puts a number on the feeling: ten times. Not once, not twice, but ten. Ten times they have insulted me. Ten times they have *shamelessly* insulted him.

Job even allows for some possible fault in himself. In Job 19:4, he basically says, "Hey, even if I have committed some error, isn't that my thing to deal with?" Maybe he has done something wrong, if so, he's willing to admit it. But he's still asking, "Is that reason for you guys to gang up on me and beat me up with your words?"

It is amazing how hurtful his friends' attempts at being helpful have been. Job is in a pile. And they are piling on.

When your world is rocked, and you are trying to find your way out, occasionally, some so-called friends are going to come with their advice and their bad doctrine and they're going to pile on, giving you all kinds of information and making all kinds of assertions that are going to make your hurt worse. I don't understand it any more than Job did. If my pain is God's plan, then let God be glorified. Why do betrayers have to use my struggle as an opportunity to be know-it-alls? Why do they have to use my setback to move themselves ahead? Why are they capitalizing on my confusion?

Job voices his frustration over this betrayal this way:

> Though I cry, "I've been wronged!"
> I get no response;

> though I call for help, there is no justice.
> He has blocked my way so I cannot pass;
> He has shrouded my paths in darkness.
> He has stripped me of my honor
> and removed the crown from my head.
> He tears me down on every side till I am gone;
> He uproots my hope like a tree.
> His anger burns against me;
> He counts me among his enemies.
> His troops advance in force;
> they build a siege ramp against me
> and encamp around my tent.
> He has alienated my brothers from me;
> my acquaintances are completely
> estranged from me.
>
> (Job 19:7-13)

Job is between a rock and a hard place, with his friends standing over him and weighing him down with their words, and he just cries out. He has to express himself. He can't keep it in. About now, Job is thinking, "God, what is up? I've had everything taken from me, and now you're preventing me from doing anything about it. On top of all that, I am deserted and betrayed by my surviving friends and family." His brothers are alienated from him. His acquaintances are estranged from him. Those relationships are broken just as his world is broken. Everything—and every*one*—has failed him.

The feeling Job is enduring is not just the raw pain of losing everything but now feeling like a total stranger. Have you ever felt like a stranger in your own house? Have you ever walked in to work and just felt as though you're a first-time guest and everyone is looking at you as though you're an alien?

My pastor told me a story about when he walked through a time of bitter betrayal. He was away from his church, out traveling and preaching. When he came back to the church, which he founded and planted, he pulled up in to his parking spot and discovered his name was no longer on a sign there. Literally, he went to his office and his name was no longer on the door. While he was gone, they had taken everything away from him.

Job continues:

> My kinsmen have gone away;
> my friends have forgotten me.
> My guests and my maidservants
> count me a stranger;
> they look upon me as an alien.
> I summon my servant,
> but he does not answer,
> though I beg him with my own mouth.
> My breath is offensive to my wife;
> I am loathsome to my own brothers.
> Even the little boys scorn me;
> when I appear, they ridicule me.

> All my intimate friends detest me;
> those I love have turned against me.
> I am nothing but skin and bones;
> I have escaped with only the skin
> of my teeth.
>
> (Job 19:14-20)

When Job's world got rocked, his entire life changed. His entire environment changed, right down to the relationships he had. Even his maids act like they don't know who he is. They treat him like a stranger. He calls for their help, and they essentially say, "Get it yourself." Job says he even begs them to help, but they don't do it. His wife treats him like he has bad breath. His brothers treat him like he's disgusting. Even the little kids are kicking him in the shins. When he gets right down to it, he's hurt and helpless and all by his lonesome, hungry for hope. "I am nothing but skin and bones."

This is what betrayal can do to you. It robs you of your reason to go on living. If there's nothing for you and *nobody* for you, what's the point? You keep pouring yourself out, but nothing and nobody is filling you up.

The Apostle Paul says speaks to this imbalance like this in 2 Corinthians 12:15, when he writes, "If I love you more, will you love me less?" If you are walking through betrayal right now, I think you need to see it is an attack by the enemy upon your devoted love. I think the better the friend you are, the purer you are in your love and in your motives and in your agenda, the greater the betrayal you will suffer. Because Satan hates purity. He hates honesty. He hates integrity. And if he can taint your love somehow, if he can get you to back off from loving people unconditionally by betraying them yourself, then he will do it.

Paul is remarking that the more he loves the Corinthians, the more it seems like they take from him. He didn't take anything from them. He didn't demand offerings. He worked hard with his own hands. But other preachers come, he said, and they rob you blind. And you put up with them, and you hate me. In what kind of world does this makes sense? It is as though the purer he wants to be—the holier, the more Christ-like—the more he suffers.

The temptation comes in that moment: Why bother? Forget it. If you can't beat 'em, join 'em.

Betrayal gives birth to all sorts of dark questions. It opens up all sorts of vengeful feelings.

But betrayal can strengthen you too. When your world is rocked and betrayal gets piled on to your pain, you can turn it to your advantage. You can find God's plan even in others' bad advice, stupid doctrine, and hurtful words.

The Blessing of Betrayal

The story of Joseph is great for showing betrayal. His own brothers tried to leave him to die and then sold him into slavery. Do you know what Joseph said at the end of this terrible journey? "You intended to harm me, but God intended it for good" (Genesis 50:20).

David says he's sitting around a table and eating in the presence of his enemies. Do you know that feeling? Maybe for you it happens every Thanksgiving or Christmas. But do you know what David says right after he makes this observation? "You anoint *my* head with oil; *my* cup overflows" (Psalm 23:5).

We see lots of stories of betrayal in the Bible. When he needed his friends and family most, Job was betrayed. But Job is going to battle through the betrayal to find the blessing.

Jesus was betrayed. His friends abandoned him, sleeping when he was praying. One of his disciples denied him, even after denying he would. One of his disciples betrayed him, turning him into the authorities for 30 pieces of silver.

This was a man whom Jesus gave responsibility to keep the finances. Judas was in Jesus' ministry. He wasn't just a random person. He was part of the ministry. He was the treasurer! Jesus knew the whole time what Judas was doing. When it came down to the last days of His ministry, as they were eating the final supper together, Jesus said that the next guy to touch the bread was going to betray Him (Mark 14:20). This tells us at the very least that the betrayal of Jesus was anticipated by Jesus, that it was part of God's plan. It would be this betrayal that would begin to fulfill the call of God and the destiny of God in Christ's sacrifice. I don't know the answer to the question, "Could Judas have repented?" That's beside the point. But I do know that the work of Judas the betrayer fulfilled a significant purpose of God.

I'm not saying God likes it. I believe God hates betrayal. But I am saying God uses it.

I do believe, in fact, that God would say to the friends who betrayed Job, "You have done him wrong. You have not spoken of me correctly. You've really messed up." But that betrayal was used by God to push Job more fully into the Father's embrace. After losing everything, Job lost everyone, but he learned to place all his trust and dependence and devotion in God alone.

Do you realize that the cross is the ultimate symbol of betrayal? The cross reveals that all of us have betrayed God. None of us is really innocent of betrayal. We were all there at Golgotha that day. We have all stood in judgment of Jesus and said in our sin "Give us Barabbas!" All have sinned. All have fallen short of the glory of God. We all are guilty. But God used our betrayal to lead Jesus to the cross where he doesn't get revenge, but instead forgives us. At the cross, Jesus takes the punishment for our betrayal, and ends up turning betrayal into blessing.

Look, if betrayal is "good" enough to happen to Jesus, you know you're not good enough to be spared. Chances are, you're already familiar with it. You probably know the bitterness of betrayal already. Can you believe that betrayal can be a blessing? Let me confess something. It's taken me ten years after a particular situation in my life to get to the place where I'm able to say that. I'm not saying betrayal becomes a blessing quickly. But I know it can and does happen.

There is a blessing in betrayal, and I'll show you how in four ways.

1. Betrayal exposes who's really around us.

First of all, betrayal removes any facades you've been living within. It took the betrayer Judas to begin to really expose what was inside Jesus' ministry. And it might take a betrayer to expose what's really going on in your life and relationships. Getting stabbed in the back will wake you up real quick. You're going to find out who your real friends are, who's really standing with you, who really loves you. You're going to find out what's really inside of you. The bottom line is that you're going to find out if God is really inside of you when you've been betrayed or when you have feelings that God has betrayed you. You're going to find out real quick if you're really, truly believing that God owns your future.

When somebody betrays you, does it become your whole life to get back at them? Do you obsess over what they did to you, whether it was yesterday or forty years ago? When you fight to let that stuff go, you're acknowledging that they don't own your future, but God does. Betrayal reveals how close you are to traitors, but your response to betrayal reveals how close *you* are to God.

God says you better let it go. He says, "Give it to me; revenge is mine" (Romans 12:19).

When Judas betrayed Jesus, he went out into the night. Jesus immediately says, "Now is the Son of Man glorified and God is glorified in him" (John 13:31). This is before the cross. This is before He dies. When Judas was exposed and ran away, Jesus said, "Now I can be glorified. Now, I can begin to live my purpose." Sometimes it takes betrayal to expose what's really real in your life.

That's why God says in Job 42:7, "After the LORD had said these things to Job, he said to Eliphaz the Temanite, 'I am angry with you and your two friends, because you have not spoken of me what is right, as my servant Job has'." You see, Job's friends thought they were "all that." They thought they had the word of the Lord. But God says it was their whole betrayal that really exposes their true hearts.

Betrayal can be a blessing when it reveals what (and who) is true around us. But there's a second way betrayal can be a blessing.

2. Betrayal connects us to Christ.

You are never more like Christ than when you're being betrayed. Assuming that you're making the right choices, betrayal connects you to Christ.

You will never feel the Bible come more alive in your life than when you're walking through a season of betrayal. The words of Scripture begin to make much more sense, the stories seem more vivid, the commands seem more important, the encouragement seems more comforting, the wisdom seems specifically designed just for you. Why? Because in betrayal you're connecting to the character of God. When you have nothing and no one to turn to, like Jesus in the wilderness, you are living on every word that comes out of the mouth of God. You're connecting to His life.

I believe that you don't become like Christ unless you go through betrayal. I believe that betrayal can connect you to Him in prayer like never before. We connect to His character. Going through betrayal is like walking in the footsteps of Jesus.

3. Betrayal can bring promotion.

When you are experiencing betrayal, one of two things will happen to you. Betrayal will either eat your lunch or it will launch you into a whole new world. When someone betrays you, whether it's at the office or in the home, despite the often unbearable pain, it can set up a success you never expected. What they mean for evil,

God means for good. They meant it to hurt you, but God means it to build your character, to prosper you in the end. In Romans 5:3-4, Paul writes, "We also rejoice in our sufferings, because we know that suffering produces perseverance; perseverance, character; and character, hope." There's a chain of success there, but it begins with suffering. So, oftentimes, your blessing is the finish line of a journey that begins with betrayal.

What you think is the period at the end of your story God says is the start of a brand new book. Betrayal sets you free from a false reality to enter into a new world of existence. You can now enter into real life, now that the scales are off your eyes to your true friends and family, and real life is always a promotion over a façade.

The God we serve is the God who carried Job through his tragedy and gave him twice as much as he ever had to begin with. Job was greater at the end of his life than he was at the beginning of his life. It took betrayal to get there.

4. Betrayal *is* a blessing.

Betrayal doesn't just lead to a blessing. It is a blessing. How? It gives us power before God. It gives us access to God. Psalm 34:18 says, "The LORD is close to the brokenhearted and saves those who are crushed in spirit." The Bible says that God listened to the prayers of Job. There's power in that access.

In Ezekiel 14:14, God was so mad at His people Israel, He says to them, "Even if Noah, Daniel and Job were with you, I wouldn't talk to you." Why was Job mentioned? Why would God include Job? What difference would Job have made? God is saying He's so angry at Israel, He doesn't even want to see their face. But He'll listen to Job. Job had the privilege of deeply knowing God.

The incredible truth is that God wants to give you power through your brokenness and even power in your betrayal. He wants to give you the power to prevail and the power to reign and the power to rule and the power to be what God has called you to be.

We are talking about some serious stuff right now. Betrayal is no small thing. If you are carrying around the sting of betrayal in your heart, it is likely a deep, deep wound. Not a scratch. A deep sore, infected and painful. I'm talking about sexual betrayal committed against you as a child. I'm talking about marital betrayal from your spouse. When your world is rocked, it doesn't rock you on a small scale. I'm talking about the sort of betrayal that robs you of your fortune, your livelihood, your innocence, your virginity, your safety, your emotional stability, your health. This is big stuff.

We serve a big God. He is an almighty God. Your world is rocked on a big scale, but God redeems his children on a big scale too. He's an eternal God. He can outlast and outperform any betrayal you face.

It's time to turn your betrayal into a blessing. Let it go. Say, "God, I'm going to trust you."

CHAPTER SIX

ENDURING

*W*hat do you want when your world is rocked? If you had to condense your answer, I bet it would be something like restoration. What we want most of all, after everything is taken away and relationships are broken, our health is fading, and our life is in turmoil, is to be fixed. We want restoration. And the only way to get there is to keep your relationship with God intact.

This is Ellyn's story:

> When I was in my freshman year of high school, I started to notice a change between my parents. Some things just seemed to be different. They didn't seem to be getting

along as well. There seemed to be a lot of tension. I had just gotten back from a two-week mission trip to Peru where we were very active with an orphanage there. I was at the mall with my friend. And then all of a sudden, I got a phone call from my mom. I knew that something was wrong. And she said, "Ellyn, I need you to come home when you get a chance." When I got home, my mom pulled me aside. She took me outside, and we sat down in the front yard. And she said, "We are going to be getting divorced, and I'm going to be moving out of the house." I felt like I was doing what I was supposed to be doing, and this terrible thing was happening to me. I was scared. I was just wondering why, wondering if I had done anything to influence it. My whole world was rocked.

There came a point where I had to decide whose house I was going to live at. I felt like I was betraying one parent if I chose the other. Right around the time that my parents first announced their divorce, I became active in the youth worship team. When I learned to let go of everything in front of the Lord and learned what worship truly meant and what worship *leading* truly meant was when I was able to let go of some things in my life and move forward with the next step that I had to take. I had a very, very strong church home and friends that were very invested in me. Nothing is impossible with God. And I still have two wonderful parents who love me very much, spend time with me and invest time into their relationships with me. I am still very, very fortunate. I was totally right to devote every bit of my time to God during my struggle. It was worth it. And it is still worth it. And I made a right decision to turn to God instead of turning to other things. And now I can impact people's lives for the better.

I remember a time my own world was rocked. My father was a coach in the NFL, which we jokingly said stood for "Not For Long." I had just returned back from the lake with a friend of ours in Atlanta. My mom picked me up at my friend's house and gave me the news that we were moving. Again. When you're young, news like that can shake you. The upheaval in your life, that everything you knew was going to change—it rocked me.

There was another time that my life was rocked and I remember it so clearly. January 10th, 1987, I was sitting on a deer stand and while waiting, something jumped on me, I had an impression in my heart that that particular day would be the greatest day of my life and I would never be the same after it. I wondered what would happen. I literally looked to heaven and asked what would happen. I had a sense that something big was shifting. I thought maybe I would kill the world's largest deer and become famous with this huge animal, but about three hours later I ended up discovering that my father had a massive heart attack. I knew instantly that it was the voice of God that had been speaking to me earlier.

I drove to the hospital and met my father coming in the ambulance. I walked into the bathroom and began to talk to the Lord. I told Him that I heard Him and I knew He had been talking to me. I asked Him to take my life and do what He wanted to with it forever. My father ended up passing away. I knew that this would be considered a horrible day in the world's eyes, and it *was* very painful for me to experience, but I knew deep down that it actually became the greatest day of my life since it was the day I began my relationship with the Lord. Our days with Jesus are the best days, but they can simultaneously be the worse days. Like Jesus said in the Beatitudes, blessed are the poor, meek, and the weak for they shall receive comfort, grace, and mercy. You've got to walk through those days of brokenness, experiencing the opposite of happiness and success, believing that God has a purpose in it and a plan for it. It takes that endurance to get a blessing sometimes. It takes trust that He will redeem what was taken. But as emotionally traumatic as that upheaval was, the upheaval in Job's life was much, much worse. It was devastating. We've seen how he's lost his business and finances, how he's lost his children, and how he's lost his health. Then he even loses the support of his wife, who nags him, and his friends, who hammer him with bad advice and bad doctrine.

The Endurance Blessing

If anybody had a case for being an agnostic or an atheist, it was Job. If anybody could say, you know, "I don't believe in this God garbage. I don't believe in it," Job could say it. If God is so good and if He's so loving and if He's so much a savior, then why is this happening? Job could have been like the millions of believers who have lost their faith, and lost their way.

Instead of changing its behavior, our generation changes its belief. We're living in a generation of people who, when things don't go according to plan, change their beliefs. We end up contaminating our beliefs. We begin to mix up faith with other teachings that sound better and feel nicer. So we keep the parts of God that we like, and we subtract the parts of God that we don't like. We add this, and we paste that, and what we end up with is a god that we have made. The Bible calls that an idol. We're finding this kind of thinking in our current generation.

Wherever you hear principles of self-help, the end of it all should be Jesus. If it begins and ends with yourself, it's not God's way. Where is Jesus in the "law of attraction?" Nothing will make you more attractive than being like Jesus. No one was more attractive than Jesus. But in today's world we cut Jesus out and paste in what we want. It all boils down to not knowing what to do or what to think when our world is rocked.

The thing we see in Job's life is that he did not alter his belief system. Job did not leave God for greener pastures when his own was torched. He didn't change his faith to a god he thought was nicer. No, instead, Job changed his behavior. In fact, it was through the very process of being rocked that Job really discovered God. He realized who God really was. In fact, he would say in Job 42:5, "You know, I used to walk with You based on what I was told about You, but now I personally have seen who You really are." There is nothing like having your world rocked and seeing God as He really is. Having everything stripped from you frees you to trust and focus more fully on God.

And *that* is when restoration begins. The Bible tells us that at the end of Job's life, he received twice as much as he had at the beginning of his life (Job 42:10). Many of us only go halfway with God and then we stop because we've been rocked. God says to the quitters, "You missed it. You missed the blessing." Because God blesses at the end. You don't get a medal halfway through a race. There are no "participation trophies" in this race. You have to cross the finish line. But you've got to run the race to finish it. And when you cross that finish line, celebration will be waiting for you.

Notice what James says about Job in the New Testament: "We consider those blessed who have persevered" (James 5:11). Those who endure get the blessing. 2 Timothy 2:12 warns us, "If we endure, we will also reign with him. If we disown him, he will also disown us." That's a reminder and a warning!

Stay in the game. Be resilient. Keep running the race. Restoration awaits you.

Many people don't get there. Many people quit their faith. They quit life. They quit the life of God. They quit church. They quit reading their Bible. They quit praying. They quit processing. They quit fighting. They quit loving.

But quitters will never find out where the blessing is. They don't endure.

If Job's story is about anything, it's about enduring to the end of a rocked world. This is what I believe God is telling us through the story of Job: You and I can be restored and receive back all that was taken from us, if we'll only go back out there and play the second half.

This is how the story of Job ends:

> After Job had prayed for his friends, the LORD made him prosperous again and gave him twice as much as he had before. All his brothers and sisters and everyone who had known him before came and ate with him in his house. They comforted and consoled him over all the trouble the LORD had brought upon him, and each one gave him a piece of silver and a gold ring.
>
> The LORD blessed the latter part of Job's life more than the first. He had fourteen thousand sheep, six thousand camels, a thousand yoke of oxen and a thousand donkeys. And he also had seven sons and three daughters. The first daughter he named Jemimah, the second Keziah and the third Keren-Happuch. Nowhere in all the land was there found women as beautiful as Job's daughters, and their father granted them an inheritance along with their brothers.
>
> After this, Job lived a hundred and forty years; he saw his children and their children

to the fourth generation. And so he died, old
and full of years.

(Job 42:10-17)

The end tells us that the Lord restored the fortunes
of Job after he prayed for his friends. The Lord increased
Job to the tune of twice as much as he had before. All of
his brothers and all of his sisters and all who had known
him before came back to him, and they had dinner with
him in his house. They consoled him and comforted him.
They even gave him some money! The Lord blessed the
latter days of Job more than he had in his early days.
He received his business back and it was bigger. He was
blessed with more children, all of them handsome and
beautiful.

Job went from utterly empty to exceedingly full. He
was lavishly blessed. He was so blessed, in fact, that he
broke tradition in that culture and gave his daughters
an inheritance just as he did his sons. You didn't give
daughters an inheritance in those days. But Job did,
because he just had so much money and felt so blessed.

And at the end of all this, Job lived 140 years after
his world was rocked. Isn't that a great answer to the
question, "Can a man live again?" Yes! For over a century

more. And when Job died, he died old and full. He didn't die empty. He didn't die broke. He didn't die in poverty. He didn't die as a beggar. He died full of life. He died restored.

Enduring to Rebuild

In the Old Testament, long after Job was alive, the wall around Israel had been demolished and the people were exiled from their land. God used a man named Nehemiah to rebuild that wall and return people to their homeland. The wall was rebuilt in 52 days. While he was repairing what had been torn down by the enemy, Nehemiah asked, "Will these stones be used again? Will they pull the stones from the rubbish and use them again?" Nehemiah's question speaks so clearly to the truth that God redeems his children out of their mess and devastation. He uses it to bring forth a testimony. Brick by brick, stone by stone, the Israelites repaired the wall.

A brick by itself is nothing, but one pulled out from the rubbish and placed in the hand of God and connected to other people becomes a testimony. Being rocked in and of itself is of no benefit, but God can pull blessing out of the rubble and rubbish, and use it. He can use your rubble to rebuild in you and for you something better. He used the stones again, and not only did he reuse the stones, he used them to rebuild the wall *quickly*.

When you are pulled out of the rubble, restored and rebuilt, you can connect other people to God. You can then be used to rescue other people, because those who are rescued can rescue. The ruined stones can and will be used again. Your life, after being rocked, can be restored and used by God in a mighty way.

Job experienced the same full restoration. His life was a testimony to all his friends of God's redeeming power.

CHAPTER SEVEN

RESTORATION

What was available to Job is available to you too. Has your world been rocked to its foundation? You can find restoration. You can find yourself back up on top again. You can get your dream back. You can get your desires back. You can walk through a painful season and experience restoration on the other side.

I believe there are five principles that will literally bring restoration into your life. They come straight from the life of Job.

1. Job was faithful.

In Job 19:25, as Job is sitting on an ash heap, literally "down in the dumps," he feels the weight of the nothingness he now has in his life, has the deep pain of grief in his heart over the loss of his children, hurts badly from the festering boils on his skin, and he says this: "I know that my redeemer lives, and that in the end He will stand upon the earth."

Sometimes—in fact, *especially*—when you are going through the dumpiest time of your life, you need to say with conviction, "I know that my redeemer lives." Notice the faith Job has in how it will all end up: At the end Jesus is going to stand on the earth. Then he says:

> And after my skin has been destroyed,
> yet in my flesh I will see God;
> I myself will see Him
> with my own eyes—I, and not another.
> How my heart yearns within me!
> (Job 19:26-27)

In other words, his heart longs for this. I want you to first see that in the midst of Job's pain, he was making a declaration that God the Redeemer is going to restore his life and do a new work in it.

If you want to be restored, it all starts with your mouth. When God wanted to restore the earth—the Bible says it was full of chaos and confusion is Genesis 1—God said, "Let there be light." And you need to say when you're in the dumps of life, when you've lost your business or you've lost your children or you've lost your body, "God, I know that you live, and as for me, I am going to see you restore my life." Don't try to wait until the pain is gone to say this. Job said it in pain. He made this declaration despite his pain.

Sometimes the last thing we want to do is say good things when we are in pain. In fact, the first thing we want to do when we're in pain is cuss a little bit, gripe a little bit, moan a little bit, murmur a little bit, get agnostic a little bit, and get atheistic a little bit. Job tosses all that aside and says, "I know my redeemer lives."

Do you know Jesus lives? Do you know God is going to take His stand in your life?

The Bible says that God was full of compassion and mercy, and Job died full. But what did he die full of? The Lord's compassion and mercy.

So if you want to begin the restoration process and you're tired of living a rocked life, you need to be faithful.

You need to be faithful to the word of God. You need to be faithful to speak the word of God. The Bible says in 1 John 5:4 that our faith helps us overcome.

When everything around you crumbles, have faith that Jesus is on the throne, still in control, and that God is working something in your life that will bring you to restoration in the end.

But Job wasn't just faithful.

2. Job was spiritual.

Now, I don't mean spiritual like those strange, self-proclaimed mind readers who are on late at night, talking to ghosts and ancestors. I don't mean "horoscope spiritual." Not "palm-reading spiritual."

Sometimes when you say to people that they need to become spiritual, in their minds it somehow means to become spooky and weird and go after things that are not biblical. When I say "spiritual," I'm talking about being full of the truth. By "spiritual," I mean realizing that the doorway into the kingdom of God begins with you saying, "Lord, I cannot be led by my flesh. I must be led by the Spirit of God."

In John 3, a religious man named Nicodemus came to Jesus and said, "Lord, I want to talk to you about the kingdom of God. I want to talk to you about what it means to be saved." Nicodemus knew Jesus was from God, and he wanted to know how to get eternal life. Jesus' response is this:

> I tell you the truth, no one can enter the kingdom of God unless he is born of water and the Spirit. Flesh gives birth to flesh, but the Spirit gives birth to spirit
> (John 3:5-6).

In other words, Nicodemus was coming to the Lord religiously and had a religious concern, but he was not being spiritual. What he wanted to do was to step into the kingdom of God in the flesh. The Bible says that flesh does not inherit the kingdom of God (1 Corinthians 15:50).

Restoration is promised to Job. But Job has to pray for his friends first. The ones who betrayed him with their stupid words. Job could have said, "I can't do that. I'm not going to do that. They don't deserve it, and I don't feel like it." Job could see that the Lord was giving him a spiritual direction to get out of his fleshly situation.

When you want to begin to see the restoration of God in your life, it will be your natural thinking to say, "I've got to make this happen. I'm going to take this in to my own hands." Just as Nicodemus had some religious plan to get to heaven, Jesus instead is saying, "It won't happen unless you're born from above." Unless you have a spiritual understanding that you cannot enter the kingdom of heaven in the flesh, you will not enter the restoration God has for you. You won't enter God's blessing as long as your mind is set on the flesh.

So God has Job take a spiritual approach to his restoration. "Pray for your friends, Job." Job's thinking, "You mean, the ones that betrayed me?" And God says, "That's exactly right."

God saw that Job was faithful, but he also called him to be spiritual. And oftentimes God asks the spiritual to do silly things. How silly is it, how *ridiculous* is it that God would ask him to pray for his fake friends! Ever felt God calling you into something spiritual that just feels silly to your flesh? You think, "This is not what I need, God. I just want all my stuff back." But God says it starts by being spiritual, by taking your mind off your natural instincts and setting them on his ways, which can often be confusing or difficult to understand.

The reason for this is that a spiritual man can receive what Christ is saying. A spiritual man can receive direction from God that doesn't make sense to the world. The Bible says the cross of Christ is foolishness to those who are perishing (1 Corinthians 1:18). To the unspiritual mind, it's moronic that a man would die on a cross. Ridiculous. Ignorant. The whole story of Christianity—that God would send his only begotten son into a sinful world so that whoever believes in him would not perish but have everlasting life—sounds idiotic. This is why the Bible says the fleshly man can't understand it. Paul says in Romans 8:5-7:

> Those who live according to the sinful nature have their minds set on what that nature desires; but those who live in accordance with the Spirit have their minds set on what the Spirit desires. The mind of sinful man is death, but the mind controlled by the Spirit is life and peace; the sinful mind is hostile to God. It does not submit to God's law, nor can it do so.

This is why when people were following after Jesus they received the fleshly food of fish and bread really easily, but stumbled on his offering of spiritual food (John 6). They were receiving from the Lord the multiplication of fish and loaves. They were having their needs met in the flesh. Then all of a sudden, the Lord brings a spiritual word and he says drink My blood and eat My flesh. They were like, "Say what?" The command to eat His flesh and drink His blood sounded ridiculous to the fleshly. The Bible says the ones who had just had their fleshly needs met walked away from Him. Thousands of people quit the church that day because He gave a spiritual direction to handle a fleshly problem.

Jesus wasn't saying, "Come here, take a bite of my arm, and if there is anything left, grab a toe." He wasn't saying that. But he was speaking in a way that would have been understood by those who were thinking spiritually. He wanted the people who were consuming the natural food He'd provided to make the connection between that filling and the filling he could provide for their spiritual needs. But they weren't spiritual enough to hear it.

The Lord wants Job to pray for his friends. That's a spiritual request to a guy who's lost natural things. What the Lord will do to recover what you've lost in your life may seem unnatural and weird, but if you are tuned into His spiritual frequency, you will obey in trust.

The Scriptures are full of stories where people were told to do silly things. In 2 Kings 13, Elisha the prophet is about to die, but he's going to share his power with King Jehoash one last time. Jehoash is troubled by the approaching enemies of Israel. So he goes to Elisha's deathbed, and Elisha the prophet says, "Take an arrow and hit the ground with it." I'm sure Jehoash was thinking that sounded really stupid. But he hit the ground with the arrow anyway, and he hit the ground three times. And then he stops. And Elisha freaks out. He says, "You dummy, you have six enemies. If you'd hit the ground with the arrow six times, all of them would have been defeated. Instead you'll only defeat three of them." Elisha had given Jehoash a spiritual key to victory, but it seemed weird and silly and unnatural, so Jehoash failed to be blessed by it.

It's our job to become spiritual in order to listen to the Spirit of God. "He who has ears, let them hear," the Bible says (Matthew 11:15). Many people miss the calling of God in their life because they're fleshly and carnal, and they don't even hear it.

God wants you to take a spiritual angle on the problem of your rocked world. He wants you to be faithful and he wants you to be spiritual. Job fulfilled both of those callings to receive restoration in his life. But Job also did something else:

3. Job was merciful.

Job couldn't pray for his bad friends begrudgingly. He couldn't go through the motions. That's not really obedience. God could see his heart. And you can't truly say, "God, be good to these people, be good to my enemies," if in your heart you really do wish them to get what's coming to them. Being faithful and spiritual can't be playing a part. You have to work them from your heart.

In all that God tells Job to do and all that He wants him to be, He's telling Job, "You're going to have to be merciful." Is God loving and compassionate? Yes. So if we're going to be holy as He is holy, like 1 Peter 1:16 tells us, we have to be loving and compassionate too.

God looks on those who are merciful and gracious and kind with favor. God says, "That's the kind of person I will look to."

When Job started praying for his friends it meant he was willing to forgive and love and be merciful to those who had hurt him deeply. It meant finding the strength somehow, even though all his strength was gone, to pour himself out for those who had not done the same for him. In Matthew 5:43-44, Jesus says, "You have heard that it was said, 'Love your neighbor and hate your enemy.' But I tell you: Love your enemies and pray for those who persecute you." Jesus turns the table on how to treat others! He takes it to a whole new level. Love your enemies and pray for them. Bless even those who have persecuted you. If you won't do that, you won't be restored. Don't say you can't do it, or God will say He can't bless you. (It suddenly makes you rethink what you can and can't do, doesn't it?) God is promising restoration. But to enter that promise, you have to obey His call to live the way He wants you to live, and because God is merciful to us in our disobedience, we are supposed to be merciful to those who do us wrong too.

Are you merciful? Are you gracious? Who is that person in your life right now, the last one on earth that you would want to be blessed? You need to bless them somehow. Doing so will be healing and freeing.

How do you handle that person you see at the grocery store or work or even church, the one you want to avoid at all costs? What happens to you when you see them? Do you melt? Do you burn with anger? Or do you say, "God, you have given me an opportunity to get them back, but I'm going to be merciful and forgiving"? That's how He restored you: by forgiving you and being merciful to you. And that's how you'll experience restoration after your world is rocked. Be merciful to others.

Like Job, be faithful, be spiritual, and be merciful. But there's a fourth principle for reaching restoration that we see in the life of Job.

4. Job was prayerful.

Nothing moves God like prayer. When Job hit the bottom, Job prayed his way up and out. Most of the entire book of Job is a long conversation between Job and God. He was praying his guts out.

Nothing will release you faster and open the windows of heaven over your prison-like situation wider like prayer.

In Acts 12, we see Peter sitting in prison. But verse 5 says the church was "earnestly praying for him." The result was his miraculous escape. When you find yourself in prison, you pray. Nothing will make you pray like prison. Nothing will bring you to your knees in prayer like being brought to your knees in pain. You're already down there. Might as well pray! Peter, like Job, found himself in a situation that he could not get out of. But prayer set him free.

Get to the point with God. Speak to God specifically about the situations concerning you. Do you know why God wants you to be specific about your requests to him? Because it takes energy. It takes time. It takes a concentrated effort to be specific. Anyone can meander and wander in prayer. Anyone can just shoot the breeze. But when you get specific, God knows you're sacrificing. When you get specific, it tells Him you're taking the time and the energy to think through what you're praying. You have resolve. The church wasn't earnestly praying for all the prisoners. I'm sure they prayed for all the prisoners every now and then and at other times, but this time, their "earnest" prayer was specifically honed in on Peter's needs. They gave God a target.

When you get specific, do you know what you're doing? You're setting the response up for the glory of God, for His answer to be unmistakable. If all the prisoners had been released, someone could have said, "Well, Peter got out because everyone got out." But praying specifically for Peter and Peter specifically being released says undeniably that God did it.

Acts 12:5 says the church prayed "earnestly" for Peter. The New American Standard Bible says they were praying "fervently." They prayed passionately. They prayed with gusto. If you were in prison, wouldn't you want someone to pray like this for you? Wouldn't you want someone crying tears for you, feeling physical aches for you, spending lots of time and energy in intercession to God for you?

Pray and don't stop. Be like the persistent widow Jesus talks about in the parable (Luke 18:1-8). She didn't give up. She kept pestering. Keep "pestering" God, keep praying with passion. The church heard that Peter was in prison and they didn't put off praying for him. They did it quickly and earnestly. They didn't go shopping first. They didn't procrastinate in their prayer. Passionately they began to cry out to God.

When you pray, don't pray with a part of your life. Pray with all your heart, with all your soul, with all your mind. When your world is rocked, get in that prayer closet with God and pray your guts out. I don't believe it takes years to get an answer from God when you give him all of your heart with immediacy.

Be specific, be passionate, and now, be direct. It means to pray specifically to God. Grab hold of that direct line. How do you approach God? In the name of Jesus.

Don't pray like, "Oh, God, the big man upstairs . . ." God is not the big grandpa up in the sky. Jesus said it clearly: Nobody goes to the Father except through Him (John 14:6). Nobody can talk to the Father except in the name of Jesus. You talk to the Father through the Son. In our day and age, from the public schools to the church house, people are being slowly shifted to believe that you can get a hold of God however you choose, as long as you're sincere. The truth is that you can be sincerely lost! There was nobody more loving than Jesus, but nobody as dogmatic as him either. He was very clear: you cannot go to the Father except through His name.

If you want to be prayerful, you better be specific, be passionate, and be direct. Job's prayerfulness was added to his faithfulness, his spirituality, and his mercifulness as the keys to his restoration. But there's a fifth and final key:

5. Job was worshipful.

Job was restored because he was worshipful. What does that mean? It means that Job did not put himself at the center of his world. He put God first. He recognized who God is and he decided to orbit around God.

If anybody needed prayer, it was Job. But Job heard God saying, "It's not about you. It's about me. It's about my word."

Worship means being willing to break until you're broken, and then staying that way. You don't get to God unless there is brokenness. And then in your brokenness, a worshipful heart says, "God, I'm in a lot of pain, but I care more about you than I do myself. To you be all the glory and the honor and the praise."

When the woman came to Jesus with a box of alabaster, she broke it (Mark 14:3-9). She didn't open it. She broke it. The perfume inside was spilled out. When you want the presence of God and the restoration process of God in your life, you have to know it entails your brokenness and being poured out. God says, "Get broken." Psalm 51:7 says, "The sacrifices of God are a broken spirit; a broken and contrite heart, O God, you will not despise." Your sacrifice from a broken spirit and a broken heart will be looked upon by God with favor, just as the Lord looked in favor upon the woman who broke open her perfume before Him.

When you worship, it says you don't care about things being "just so." They're not that way when your world is rocked, anyway. When things are fallen apart, it doesn't make sense to try to keep everything together by your own hand. You're not that strong. When things begin to break, that's your cue to break your heart open on the mercy of God.

A worshipful heart says, "I seek you first, God." Worship says, "I'm not concerned with myself, but I'm concerned with God." Get to the place where you can say, "Father, it is not about me. It's about your word, and it's about your world."

When Job came to the point where he prayed for his friends and felt merciful toward them, when he came to the point of placing his broken heart on the altar before God, that was the point at which God restored him. You can experience this same restoration, beginning today, if you will walk in these principles.

God is saying to you, "I am not going to start the release from your prison cell until you center on Me."

When your world is rocked, you will be tempted to think and act and feel as though the world revolves around you. But it doesn't. All things were made by Him and for Him. He is supreme over all things and He holds them together (Colossians 1:17).

Do you want to be restored? Are you willing to do what Job did? Are you willing today to move back to your faith, back to the truth that your redeemer lives?

Maybe you've lost your faith. Maybe you've lost your way. Christ today is calling you back to Him. Your world may be rocked from top to bottom, but restoration awaits you in His arms.

Do you struggle with bitterness? Do you struggle with betrayal? Do you struggle with prayer? Whatever your struggles, Jesus says, "Come to Me all who are weary and burdened, and I will give you rest" (Matthew 11:28).

If you will honor God with the faithful application of what we have learned from the life of Job, He will honor you with abundant restoration. You *can* live again. That is His promise to you.

And you can start living today.

CONCLUSION

Yes, God's promise to you is that you can start living today, while it is still called "today," as the author of Hebrews encourages us (Hebrews 3:13).

One thing I could do in these final pages is try to put a neat and tidy ribbon on the concept of having your world rocked. But nobody can wrap a tidy bow on your pain. Nobody can "pretty up" the remains of your rocked world. The truth is, though, that God can help you see your trials as a gift. He can help you see that having your world rocked can be just as great an opportunity as it is a devastation. We see this most vividly in Jesus' sacrificial death itself. Crucifixion isn't pretty. There's nothing "inspirational" about Jesus being tortured and nailed to a cross. And yet in being murdered on a cross,

Jesus was actually conquering sin and brokenness. When His killers lifted him up to die, they were lifting Him up as an emblem of our healing.

That is a strange thing to think about, but it's true that God uses our pain to make us like Jesus, and that somehow, in the big scheme of God's purposes, He is working our rocked world for good. Like a blacksmith places a piece of metal in the damaging heat of fire and then hammers against it on the anvil to mold it to the right shape, God may use our painful experiences to shape us into stronger, wiser, more resilient, and more faithful people.

Your trial may not be over by the time you close this book. I hope you have found great encouragement from the story of Job and plenty of practical ways to navigate through the ruins of a rocked world. But I also hope you have learned that God is in the midst of your brokenness. He is near to you. He cares about you. He loves you. He sent his Son to die for you, and His Son didn't stay dead! He rose from the dead and was exalted to the right hand of God for you. And He sends his Spirit to be your comforter, your teacher, and your helper.

God has not abandoned you, even if everyone and everything else has. Job 36:15 tells us, "But by means of their suffering, He rescues those who suffer." So even in your pain, God is at work in you. Your world can't be rocked to an extent that God can't handle. Between his almighty power and His faithful love, He has you covered. Psalm 51:17 says that He doesn't reject the broken hearted. This is the exact moment you should draw near to Him.

Sometimes the best thing children of God can keep in mind when the world comes crashing down is that we aren't made for this world. What is happening to us now, as devastating as it can be and as hopeless as it may seem, is still temporary in the grand scheme of things. All that God allows to rock us in this life is preparing our hearts for the life to come.

The lessons in this book can help you turn your heart more and more to trust the God who made you and loves you and has a plan for your success, in this life and the next. My prayer for you is that if right now you are overwhelmed by pain or destruction, you will feel overwhelmed by God's love for you.

> Give your burdens to the Lord,
> and he will take care of you.
> He will not permit the godly to slip and fall.
> (Psalm 55:22)